Action versus Contemplation

WHY AN ANCIENT DEBATE STILL MATTERS

Jennifer Summit & Blakey Vermeule

The University of Chicago Press

Chicago and London

The University of Chicago Press, Chicago 60637
The University of Chicago Press, Ltd., London
© 2018 by The University of Chicago
All rights reserved. No part of this book may be used or reproduced
in any manner whatsoever without written permission, except in the
case of brief quotations in critical articles and reviews. For more
information, contact the University of Chicago Press,
1427 East 60th Street, Chicago, IL 60637.
Published 2018
Printed in the United States of America

27 26 25 24 23 22 21 20 19 18   1 2 3 4 5

ISBN-13: 978-0-226-03223-8 (cloth)
ISBN-13: 978-0-226-03237-5 (e-book)
DOI: https://doi.org/10.7208/chicago/9780226032375.001.0001

Library of Congress Cataloging-in-Publication Data
Names: Summit, Jennifer, author. | Vermeule, Blakey, author.
Title: Action versus contemplation : why an ancient debate still matters /
Jennifer Summit, Blakey Vermeule.
Description: Chicago ; London : The University of Chicago Press, 2018. |
Includes bibliographical references and index.
Identifiers: LCCN 2017042173 | ISBN 9780226032238 (cloth : alk. paper) |
ISBN 9780226032375 (e-book)
Subjects: LCSH: Life. | Meaning (Philosophy) | Ideals (Philosophy)
Classification: LCC BD435 .S798 2018 | DDC 128/.4—dc23
LC record available at https://lccn.loc.gov/2017042173

♾ This paper meets the requirements of ANSI/NISO Z39.48-1992
(Permanence of Paper).

Contents

Introduction

Once upon a time there were some ants. They gathered food all summer and laid up stores for the winter. The ants were small, but they worked together so that everyone would have enough for the long season ahead. Meanwhile, their neighbor, the grasshopper, spent the summer hopping in the sun. "Winter is coming," they warned him. "You'd better prepare!" The grasshopper just laughed: "I live in the moment. You should stop to enjoy life, too, rather than wasting it in mindless work!" But the ants just worked harder. When winter came, the ants settled in with their supplies, and the grasshopper had nothing. Hungry and cold, he turned to his neighbors for help. But they had only enough for themselves and nothing to spare. "In the summer it looked like we were wasting our lives," the ants told him. "Now you know that we were saving them."

· · ·

Once upon a time, there were some ants, who spent the fine summer of their short and precious lives toiling in Pharaoh's army, marching robotically to the monotonous beat of the same tinny drum. Unable to think for themselves, much less to suck the marrow out of life, they worshipped such dreary, neoliberal quasi-virtues as "efficiency," "outcomes," and the corporate ethos. They hired consultants and put stopwatches on the shop floor. The grasshopper was appalled. Nobody in ant-world ever seemed to have a free moment to think or reflect, much less to play or enjoy. Efficient they might be, but they were hardly creative and far from happy. As for laying up stores for the winter, surely, thought the grasshopper, it is better to be happy now and play catch-as-catch-can later.

. . .

Some stories work their way into the collective consciousness and never really leave. The ant and the grasshopper come to us from antiquity.[1] Yet they are hardly just characters in an agrarian tale about the need to be prudent during times of feast in anticipation of coming famine, a story that would have made much more sense to our chronically hungry ancestors than to our overfed selves. Rather, they represent, in the words of William Blake, "two contrary states of the soul." The ant and the grasshopper personify traits possessed by *all* people: the urge to step back, to consider our shortness of life and smallness in the cosmos, to experience life rather than waste it, versus the need to act in service of a greater good, to contribute to something bigger than ourselves, to help others endure the struggles we all share. Most of us experience both impulses regularly—sometimes in conflict, sometimes intertwined.

Yet the story as it has come down to us has a harsh moral: live like an ant or die like a grasshopper. Work for the future or find yourself in a desperate pass. The choice is starkly clear. In our lived experience, by contrast, it is downright murky. We aspire—not often successfully—to finding grasshopper-like enjoyment and fulfillment in our daily work. And even the most ant-like among us can't easily square the ants' virtuous work ethic with their lack of charity. Yet as children, we learn to see work and pleasure through the divisive lens of either/or.

The story of the ant and the grasshopper has woven itself tightly into the fabric of the modern mind. Around this fable cluster many of our culture's most pressing myths, conversations, and collective freak-outs. (Remember the "tiger mother" and the howling that went up when she claimed that Asian children are more successful than other children because non-Asian, and especially white, parents indulge their children rather than teaching them discipline?)[2] The fable concerns itself, rather primally, with character development, which is central to child rearing—two areas flooded by rivers of advice, much of it quite harsh and moralizing and scary. We do not offer much advice in this book. Rather we offer a larger intellectual context for the ant and the grasshopper, and the issues that fable brings to life. This context is the ancient debate between the active life and the contemplative life.

For four years, we taught a freshman lecture course at Stanford University called "A Life of Action or a Life of Contemplation: Debates in Western Literature and Philosophy." The syllabus evolved with the course, but a core set of questions remained constant: Which is more valuable, knowledge or action? Which is the greater achievement, wisdom or material success? What is best, a life of active accomplishment or a life of spiritual or intellectual contemplation? Are action and contemplation necessarily at odds, or can we hope to achieve a balance between them?

These questions concern the essence of a life well lived, a subject our students were eager to debate. But the point of our course, and now of this book, is also to show that the debate over the relative value of the *vita activa* and the *vita contempla-tiva*, tenaciously waged since ancient times, has a fresh urgency in the twenty-first century. The central terms of this opposition—action versus thought, skill versus knowledge, worldly engagement versus otherworldly reflection—have persisted across time even as their forms and implications have changed. The classical, medieval, and early modern periods shaped the debate's foundational questions: What is the measure of a life well lived, our acts or our strength of spirit? Are we more likely to find wisdom in solitude or in the company of others? How do we balance the demands of charity with those of religious or philosophical reflection? Modernity viewed these questions through the lens of Cartesian dualism, with its opposition of the material body to the immaterial mind, and adapted them to the challenging realities of the industrial and post-industrial eras, whose values are so conspicuously material. Even in this context, the opposition of active and contemplative lives, instead of producing resolution, generates more questions: Who are we, beyond what we make and what we do? What is the use of thought, knowledge, and truth in an age that measures value in terms of productivity? What forms of intelligence does capitalist modernity reward, and why? How else might we define our life's value?

These questions have been debated and refined in the works of the world's great thinkers: Plato and Aristotle, Shakespeare and Thoreau, George Eliot and Hannah Arendt. But they are also intimately, uncomfortably familiar to our students as they choose courses, declare fields of study, and attempt to chart their own paths. We hoped that our course would help them to perceive and explore the philosophical roots of practical questions they confront every day: Should you pick your major based on your interests or on its potential financial return? When is it better to socialize than to study? Should you get a job after graduation or stay in school for another degree? What is college for, anyway? If, as many writers have argued, the Anglo-American university has become an adjunct of the labor market, and thus of private corporations, self-examination will increasingly have to do with the question of how to fashion a self in a market-dominated world.[3]

Many students have told us that the course helped them reflect on, and even break from, the pre-professional culture and anxious résumé building that has become so widespread on American campuses since 2008. Some told us that the course had challenged them to think in new ways about their studies, their professional plans, and what mattered most to them. Yet other students had trouble seeing how the course was relevant: the debate between action and contemplation seemed out of date—"antique," as one of them wrote—not in sync with their experience of trying to stay "on track." Each of these responses told us that the course had hit a nerve, that it identified a problem that remained as alive to our students as it was to the authors and thinkers we studied, men and women who negotiated the conflicting calls of utility and meaning, productivity and purpose, as living challenges.

And our students weren't the only ones feeling this tension: we found ourselves being asked about the action/contemplation debate, on and off campus, by friends, colleagues, alumni, and family—people who felt that it described acute conflicts in their own lives. We experienced such tensions ourselves. When we first taught the course, we were two newly tenured literature professors at a research university with plentiful resources—a position about as close to the contemplative vocation as modernity allows. Yet along with the freedom to contemplate, the security of tenure brought a sense of responsibility to act, to confront questions that had become increasingly uncomfortable for both of us. We saw fewer and fewer students choosing to major in English and the other humanities, and wondered how we could articulate the value of these seemingly impractical fields—or if we should, given the insecure workplace our graduates faced. We saw our own PhD students failing to find tenure-track jobs, and questioned how, or whether, the academic humanities could adapt to the changing landscape of American higher education. We took a hard look at our own careers and the values that drove them. As educators, we urged our students to live lives of meaning and value, but could we be certain that we were attaining that goal? Given the insecurity of the post-2008 world and the inequities it produced and exposed—and our shared commitment to higher education as a force for social good and transformation—were we making the most of our positions to advance the shape and cause of knowledge in a distracted and unjust world, or were we enjoying a luxurious shelter from a world we could not change or understand?

Spending years with Plato, Shakespeare, and George Eliot in the company of hundreds of bright young people can lead to hard questions like these—questions of more than academic interest. As our encounter with these questions deepened—and with it, our appreciation of the richness of the active life/contemplative life debate—we answered them in different ways, in our lectures and in our lives. We found ourselves drawn to a wider range of sources—not just the literary classics in which we had both been trained, but research on the brain and behavior that illuminated the question from other fields, as well as film, social history, and current events that demonstrated its pervasiveness. And we made choices that changed the course of our own professional and personal lives. One of us, whose schol-

arly work had engaged the pragmatist tradition, was deeply
drawn to contemplation as a practice and a challenge to modern values. The other, who had long studied the contemplative
tradition as a scholar, was so drawn to the human connection
and contribution of the active life that she left Stanford to become an administrator at a large, public university, San Francisco State. Convinced, in the end, that this question is too vital
to be confined to the archives or the classroom, we decided to
write this book.

This topic has no ending, no fixed point on which to rest.
The debate between the active and the contemplative life runs
through the history of Western philosophy and literature like a
river, ever present and ever changing. Probably the most striking thing about the debate is that it should never have started.
Aristotle should have ended it before it began. At the mouth of
this long river stands a boulder, massive, imposing, and made of
the hardest adamantine: Aristotle's defense of contemplation in
the *Nicomachean Ethics*. Artistotle says directly and clearly that
contemplation (the Greek word is *theoria*) is the highest state of
human flourishing (*eudaimonea*). Contemplation is the highest
human good because it is "self-sufficient," "continuous" ("we
are more capable of continuous study" than of any other sort
of activity), and complete on its own: unlike most actions we
undertake, contemplation "aims at no end beyond itself."[4] We
do it for its own sake.[5] Therefore it is the most perfect of the
virtues and the most conducive to happiness.

Yet Aristotle also differentiates fulfilled happiness (*eudaimonia*) from virtue (*aretê*), doing the right thing, which proceeds
from actions and behaviors. And he concedes that *knowing* the
good (the aim of the philosopher) and *doing* the good (the aim of
the citizen) are not always necessarily aligned.[6] Indeed, the distance between knowing and doing, philosophy and citizenship,

would trouble Aristotle's followers for generations and drive a wedge between the active life and the contemplative life.

Many generations after Aristotle, the choice of the contemplative life over the active life needed active defending. When John Milton, the seventeenth-century English poet, was in his early twenties, he wrote two poems, "L'Allegro" (the happy man, the active type) and "Il Penseroso" (the thoughtful man, the contemplative type). At least on the surface, the happy man seems to have much the better lot in life. He plans to dance and drink and carouse and have a carefree time with "mirth and youthful jollity." The thoughtful man, by contrast, grinds away in a state of morally strenuous solitude, his surroundings dark and gloomy. Although drawn to "the busie humm of men" like the social partisan of the active life, L'Allegro looks like the grasshopper, given over to a life of "unreproved pleasures free." In contrast, Il Penseroso, who shuns human activity and "the noise of folly," looks more like the pleasure-spurning ants; yet he proclaims himself to be a follower of "the Cherub Contemplation."[7] Clearly for Milton, the rigorous *vita contemplativa* is the harder path to follow; the *vita activa*, the easier and alluring one.

But there is an autobiographical twist. When Milton wrote these poems, he was about to embark upon nearly a decade of "studious retirement" in the countryside. He wanted to pursue what he felt was his calling to become a poet—ultimately, the greatest epic poet in the English language. His intense ambition put him at odds with the friends he had known in college, and he was defensive about his choice of life.[8] This may help explain why, in these paired poems, Milton tips the scales in favor of the contemplative life.

Milton may have had in mind an imaginary interlocutor such as Socrates debates in Plato's dialogue *Gorgias*. There, a strong antagonist named Callicles speaks passionately, arrogantly, and decisively about the benefits of the active over the contemplative life. Philosophical contemplation, Callicles argues, is a suitable pastime for young adults to help cultivate and polish them, but it is hardly a respectable choice of life for adults: "When I see an older man still engaging in philosophy and not giving it up, I think such a man by this time needs a flogging. For, as I was just now saying, it's typical that such a man, even if he's naturally very well favored, becomes unmanly and avoids the centers of his city and the marketplaces . . . and, instead, lives the rest of his life in hiding." Socrates replies, "I disregard the things held in honor by the majority of people, and by practicing truth I really try, to the best of my ability, to be and to live as a very good man, and when I die, to die like that. And I call on all other people as well, as far as I can . . . to this way of life."[9]

The young Milton did not have a Socrates to defend him; nor does he defend his "manliness" with Socrates's vigor. Instead, he defends his choice of contemplation over action by insisting that his avoidance of pleasurable activity and dedication to rigorous contemplation will pay off far in the future, in "something like prophetic strain."[10] At the end of his career, he returns to this prophecy and judges it fulfilled. In so doing, he reasserts the value of inactivity as the greater virtue: "They also serve who only stand and wait."[11] Yet Milton's defensiveness remains palpable in that self-justifying "also." Contemplation and inactivity could find value only as an alternate form of rigorous work, just as waiting, if it could be counted as a virtue, had to look like work, not philosophical reflection.

In contemporary American life, delayed gratification has come to count as what we call "character." In the late 1960s, a Stanford psychologist named Walter Mischel began to perform an ingenious experiment that has had a long and highly moralized afterlife. He offered four-year-olds a choice: if they could wait until he came back into the room, they could have two marshmallows; if they couldn't wait, they could ring a bell and he would give them one. He then timed them to see how long they could wait to ring the bell.[12] Fifteen years later, he sent a questionnaire to the children's parents asking them a range of questions about their children's aptitudes and activities. The results were striking:

> The lengths of time the 4 year olds were able to delay [ringing the bell] were clearly linked to indexes of their cognitive competence as adolescents and young adults. For example, seconds of preschool delay time significantly predicted verbal and quantitative scores on the SAT administered in adolescence. It also correlated significantly with parental ratings of competencies, including ability to use and respond to reason, planfulness, ability to handle stress, ability to delay gratification, self-control in frustration situations, and ability to concentrate without becoming distracted.[13]

In other words, by the age of four, the extent to which people can exercise self-control in the face of obvious temptation predicts much of their future success in life, including whether they will be admitted to a good college. It looks as though character (or brain development) is destiny.

Delayed gratification defines a peculiarly American virtue, which is bound up with the relative values of the active life and the contemplative life. The Protestant work ethic came to associate work with virtue and leisured contemplation with dissolute vice. Unsurprisingly, "The Grasshopper and the Ants" would become a staple in early American primers, which taught the young how to read and write while delivering edifying lessons like that of the indignant ants: "We cannot help those who do not help themselves." Mischel's young subjects display the same virtue through similar feats of self-discipline. Eat the marshmallow now, lose two marshmallows later. Whether their choices reflect rote learning or genetic good fortune, they are worthy inheritors of the ants.

Milton was writing on the cusp of a sea change in sensibilities. His poems took the form of a debate because that was standard practice for the school exercises of his day, but they nonetheless capture an emerging, indeed modern, sensibility.[14] Ancient writers saw action and contemplation as reciprocal and complementary. They asked how people could fashion a life rich in both worldly engagement and philosophical reflection. The question persisted throughout the medieval and early modern periods, when Christian thinkers spiritualized it, aspiring to lives that balanced the imperative of prayerful reflection with day-to-day demands, whether in the cloister or in the household.

But the two lives became increasingly separated and polarized in later modernity, as the active life was perceived to crowd out the contemplative or to eliminate it completely. Milton's youthful poems seize on several psychic elements that will play an outsize role in the action/contemplation debate over the next two centuries. Action and contemplation are imagined as separate, somewhat opposed states of the human soul. To choose one is to banish the other; to live in the bright blaze of the active life is to paint the contemplative life as a patch of psychic darkness.

In contemporary society, any sense of balance or complementarity between action and contemplation has long since receded. The most visible manifestations of our twenty-first-century culture celebrate action—and not just action but *frenzy*. Contemplative practices may be available as a kind of personal virtue, but few institutions support them. They cannot afford to. The pace of competition between firms, industries, and even whole economies requires that managers demonstrate tangible results. Time scales speed up dramatically, with what counts as a result measured in shorter and shorter terms. Our era is defined by "present shock"—the sense, writes Douglas Rushkof, who coined the term, that "our society has reoriented itself to the present moment. Everything is live, real time, and always-on. It's not a mere speeding up. . . . It's more of a diminishment of anything that isn't happening right now—and the onslaught of everything that supposedly is."[15] To the extent that we submit to this reality, we ignore its very intense and real costs. As Seneca put it, "delight in bustling is not energy—it is only the restless energy of a hunted mind."[16]

All of this leads to a painful paradox. Even as we worship action, we are collectively anxious about its excesses. Among the many messages blaring at us from our digital surroundings is a persistent warning: the pace of our busy lives puts our well-being at risk. Distraction, compulsive social networking, saturation by streams of images and sounds—every part of the media- and technology-driven industrial world catches us in its mad swirl. We hear about the end of reading, the end of solitude, the end of long-form journalism, and other cultural catastrophes that will follow. While modern life acquires byzantine layers of complexity, periodic shocks in industrial capitalism have left us holding underwater mortgages, doubting the value of our pensions, and regretting the conditions that led us to live life as such a fast-paced competitive race.

So the dream of escaping to simpler and slower places or times persists: the popularity of yoga, meditation classes, and spa retreats shows that we avidly seek contemplative release, even if we remain unsure how to incorporate them into our busy lives. More often than not, we experience the desire for contemplation and the need for action to be in conflict, two competing and agonistic impulses. And our collective anxiety grows more intense when we think about the possibility that we, or somebody we care about, might fall off the ever-quickening treadmill.

Perhaps we return to the literary history of this conflict because we see in our own lives that its lessons are easier to teach than to practice. A young man came to one of us one spring and confided that he was thinking of "stopping out" of school. Not dropping out, but leaving for a while to learn permaculture farming in rural northern California. This straight-A student felt that the paper chase was draining the joy from learning. He was burned out. He had worked intensely in high school and done well in scholarship and sports. Now he wanted to work with his hands, to "make his body hard, his heart soft," as he wrote in an email. Stanford was willing to allow him a leave of absence, but his friends and family were worried. What if he got off track and never got back on? What if he lost the motivation to get his degree? I found myself joining the chorus of naysayers. I too worried that he would get lost in the wilds of Humboldt County. But none of us needed to worry. The student went to Humboldt County. He came back a year later having learned a few things about farming and a few more about human nature that he probably would not have learned had he stayed on campus. He went on to study in Australia and Chile. And to this day I regret having pressured him to stay "on track." After all, I was lecturing on Thoreau and Emerson, who talk about making your own path by walking. Yet the idea that he would get off his assigned track—the track young people and their families strive so mightily to get on—gave me a mild sense of panic.

I wanted our student to be more like the ant and less like the grasshopper. In his own way, of course, he was laying up stores for the future. In fact, he was doing a better job of preventing future regrets than I was of advising him on how to prevent them. In the short run, people may regret not having kept their noses to the grindstone. But the further they get from college, the more alumni regret not having taken more pleasure in the experience. By the time they reach middle age, they mostly regret having had "too much self control" and "missing out."[17] The grasshopper turns out to have the greater wisdom.

Up the freeway from Stanford at San Francisco State, a large comprehensive university like those attended by most American college students, the problem of students "stopping out" and getting "off track" generates panic of a different sort. With a six-year graduation rate of just over 50 percent (and a four-year graduation rate of around 20 percent), SF State students' levels of achievement fall closer to the national average than do Stanford students'. Another difference from Stanford is that students who leave are unlikely to return. Legislators, administrators, and the booming ed-tech industry specializing in keeping students on track equate "student success" with continuous enrollment and timely graduation—a goal that students and their parents understandably share, given the growing wage gap between those who earn college degrees and those who don't, who are far less likely to reach the middle class.[18] SF State students are also less likely to have advisors in whom to confide their desire to "stop out." But are they less deserving of the self-exploration and reflection that our Stanford student desired—and the benefits it turned out to provide for his educational and professional path? The right to contemplation is unevenly distributed, and with it, the right to an education that allows for reflection, self-knowledge, and personal growth.

Ironically, what makes students more likely to drop out

without completing their degrees is the choice of the wrong major. Conventional wisdom—that the earlier students declare a major, the likelier they are to persist—has made many campuses insist that students declare a major, or at least an intended major, when they first enroll. But beginning college students—particularly those who are the first in their family to attend college—have little knowledge to inform their choice. Many declare majors that appear practical, such as business or nursing. But the crowded enrollments of these programs—along with the rigors of their required courses—make them especially difficult to navigate, leading to some of the highest attrition rates on American campuses. What these students little suspect—because they are unlikely to hear it from their families or from the popular press—is that they would be more likely to thrive, both on campus and after graduation, if they selected humanities degrees that they may not have considered or even heard of.

Anytime a cost-benefit analysis is run on education, the humanities seem to come out on the wrong end. As our popular press debates whether higher education is a bubble, whether colleges are worth the cost, and how best to prepare students to navigate choppy economic waters, politicians have made something of a sport of mocking humanities degrees.

President Obama famously said, "I promise you, folks can make a lot more, potentially, with skilled manufacturing or the trades than they might with an art history degree."[19] In so saying, he was following a well-established script—a script that ignores data consistently showing that liberal arts majors tend to flourish in midcareer, while their more narrowly trained specialist peers lack the flexibility to adapt to changing work. Indeed, employers actively seek people who can speak and write clearly, who are flexible and adaptive. A 2010 survey of CEOs around the world and across industries identified creativity—

including comfort with ambiguity—as the most important factor in developing successful companies.[20] The qualities that the liberal arts foster make their graduates more likely to move into management positions than their more narrowly trained peers. English majors are more likely to gain admission to graduate business programs than are undergraduate business majors, and nurses with a liberal arts education show lower patient casualty rates than those without.

Yet the presumed opposition between the humanities and the practical world of work persists, in part due to the rhetorical self-fashioning of humanists themselves. In an 1847 letter to the secretary of his Harvard class, Henry David Thoreau resists the request to supply details of his professional activities after graduation:

> I have found out a way to live without what is commonly called employment or industry attractive or otherwise. Indeed my steadiest employment, if such it can be called, is to keep myself at the top of my condition, and ready for whatever may turn up in heaven or on earth. For the last two or three years I have lived in Concord woods alone, something more than a mile from any neighbor, in a house built entirely by myself.

Yet he insists that his way of life yields greater riches than those of his more conventionally successful classmates: "I beg that the Class will not consider me an object of charity, and if any of them are in want of pecuniary assistance, and will make known their case to me, I will engage to give them some advice of more worth than money."[21]

Advice of more worth than money? What could that be? Thoreau doesn't say directly, but we can speculate. Even though his own friends saw him less as a sage than as a bit of a tease and a misfit, Thoreau has been raised to the pantheon of great advice givers. Many a graduation speech has been shaped around his maxims: "march to the beat of a different drummer" or "suck the marrow out of life." And despite two years spent living by himself on Walden Pond, Thoreau was a trader and practical economist whose monetary calculations were as precise as the point of a sharpened pencil, the product his family manufactured. Still he might have told his penniless classmates to cultivate their minds, just as his beloved Virgil imagined cultivating a patch of land in the *Georgics*, a poem Thoreau loved.[22]

When Thoreau graduated from Harvard in 1837, only a small fraction of privileged men were expected to attend college.[23] Since then, the demographics and economics of higher education have changed drastically, as have students' academic goals and financial needs. Today a dismissal like Thoreau's of "what is commonly called employment or industry" would be an affront to most college students, who find it hard to afford college dorms, let alone a cottage in the woods. Still, the assumption that the value of higher education can be measured only in starkly pecuniary terms deserves a thoughtful response.

Arthur Zajonc, a longtime professor of physics at Amherst College and an advocate of mindfulness practice in education, visited Stanford in 2010 to moderate a dialogue with the Dalai Lama at the Center for Compassion and Altruism Research and Education. While there, he spoke to our class about contemplation as an educational goal. The financial crisis of 2008 was very much on students' minds. One freshman asked him how he could recommend mindfulness practices to students who would likely struggle to get jobs? Lurking behind the question lay a worry that contemplation would make one unfit for an intensely competitive economic environment.

Zajonc answered that practicing mindfulness is the best way we have to overcome the persistent illusion that the best response to a scarcity of resources, apparent or real, is to turn against each other. As he put it later in an email:

> If we had a stronger compassionate basis for our economic life, then scarcity and competition would make way for mutual concern and care. The cultivation of our capacity for compassion... is essential if we are to move from pieties to practice. We may understand the ideal of compassion, but we can integrate it into our lives by rehearsing compassionate feelings and action in contemplative exercises. Then, when confronted with real-world situations calling for compassionate action we are inwardly prepared.[24]

For Zajonc, crucially, contemplation does not require a withdrawal from society—neither Milton's "studious retirement" nor Thoreau's cottage in the woods. Instead, it establishes the basis of a new social ethos. By challenging the borders that divide us—like the grasshoppers from the ants—he also challenges the borders within us that frame our desires for meaningful reflection and for value-led action as in opposition. In this book, we intend to follow suit, to consider how the modern division of action and contemplation no longer applies to the world in which we, and our students, find ourselves.

· · ·

Many writers who defend the contemplative life not only accept that contemplation and action are opposing forces but become scolds, condemning modernity for letting the contemplative life become so marginal.[25] We take a different tack. Rather

than championing the contemplative life over the active—
reinforcing the idea that the two are forever in conflict—we seek
to establish the relevance and continuity of the ancient debate
in forms that still resonate in a vibrant and honest way to our
overstimulated modern brains.

As we have been suggesting, and will argue in the chapters to
come, it is a misleading and dangerous illusion to treat "action
versus contemplation" as an either/or proposition. Action and
contemplation have only intermittently been enemies. They are
vibrantly alive in each of us, potentially fused rather than sun-
dered. Some religious orders are devoted to action, whereas
some professions are highly contemplative. Even now in the
modern university, basic research in the sciences is much less
utilitarian than other parts of the STEM complex, such as engineering. Deep human needs call forth both possibilities. These
poles can turn in harmony or they can rage apart.

The relation between action and contemplation did not
spring fully formed from the modern mind. By restoring its long
and lively history, we hope to correct the view that the sudden
ascendance of the active over the contemplative life is inevitable. In the long dance between the *vita activa* and the *vita contemplativa*, the only truly unchanging element is that they call
each other forth. Mapping their history, we'll show, allows us
to see our own action-obsessed era as historically contingent.
Answering notions that the life of action is inevitably central
and that of contemplation marginal and irrelevant, we aim to
recover moments where Western intellectual and spiritual traditions have integrated the two. Such moments provide models
for redefining the challenge of balance in our lives today. Rather
than playing one against the other, we can discover how the two
nourish, invigorate, and give meaning to one another.

Nowadays some of the most explicit talk about the active

life and the contemplative life can be found in the writings of Catholic theologians and priests. Martin Laird, for example, writes movingly about prayer as a mindfulness practice. But we are not theologians. We come to our materials from our background and training as literary scholars. Our subject matter is rhetoric and stories. What we find astonishing is how many of the most charged debates in the contemporary world unconsciously draw on the rhetoric of action and contemplation: debates about work and education, money and business, science and happiness, spiritual fulfillment, and, especially, what Michel de Montaigne called the question of questions, "how to live."[26] The rhetoric of action and contemplation is nothing less than the unacknowledged medium of self-understanding in the modern world.

We have said that this is not a book of advice. Nor is it a defense of the humanities as they are currently practiced in universities and colleges in North America. It may at times seem that "the contemplative" is shorthand for "the humanities" or "the liberal arts," but that is not our claim. The academic humanities are a diverse set of disciplines with their own core principles, histories, and often intense internal debates. Several excellent books about the humanities have been written in the last few years, books that deconstruct the current landscape, place the humanities in a wider intellectual history, and defend the need for a well-functioning democracy to encourage its citizens in the byways of a liberal education. Our book does not go over that terrain again. Yet, in a few ways, the debate between the active and the contemplative life is deeply connected to the academic humanities.

The humanist tradition is reflective, as in stepping back and questioning one's assumptions. That often means delving into the history of a topic. As an example: "Accounting is a trade," writes Louis Menand, "but the history of accounting is a subject of disinterested inquiry—a liberal art. And the accountant who knows something about the history of accounting will be a better accountant." Often the liberal arts go further than this, adopting a skeptical, or indeed, oppositional, stance toward received ideas and ruling ideologies. Whether humanists take that further step toward radical critique is a matter of personal preference. But for most humanists, reflection on, as Menand puts it, "the contingency of present arrangements" is the first and necessary step.[27]

The apparent imbalance between the active and the contemplative is indeed a "present arrangement" and indeed "contingent"—meaning that it could always be otherwise and *will* be otherwise in other times and places. So our book is humanist in the sense that we invite reflection on a set of circumstances that make many people feel hopeless and trapped. And by inviting reflection, we also invite the possibility for change.

Our book is humanist in a deeper sense as well: we believe in the power of stories both as a medium and as a cure. The ascendancy of the ant in our current culture may signal the triumph of practical work over an array of impractical pursuits now embodied in the grasshopper—including literature, art, and other traditionally humanistic objects. But the continued circulation of "The Grasshopper and the Ants" suggests otherwise. The fact that the fable continues to speak to us—in ways we will delve into in chapter 4—testifies to the relevance of stories, along with the plasticity that makes it possible for them to speak across generations, through myriad forms and with changing meanings. "The Grasshopper and the Ants" carries, and has carried, many meanings over its long life. But one of them is not the irrelevance of art—in fact, just the opposite. The fable shows that art is the most powerful medium for the stories we can't quite get out of our heads. Here lies a paradox: when we claim that the ant represents the ascendance of "practical" work over "impractical" leisure, we back the fable's implicit assertion that stories capture a culture's meanings, even when they seem to reject stories themselves. If the grasshopper is a purveyor of literature, then he is the ultimate victor in the fable. But instead we would be right to see the fable as the embodiment of a dynamic, continued tension, not a zero-sum choice. It is a story that tells us that stories are good for nothing—and in the process, asserts that they are good for a great deal, for the meanings we give to our culture and our lives.

In this book, we will examine a wide range of stories—from classical literature and philosophy to present-day films, comics, and popular culture—that illustrate how relevant the living debate continues to be. Throughout, we refuse the easy bait of championing either ant or grasshopper over the other—even though the terms of the debate continually tempt us to do so. Instead, we seek counternarratives that allow us to perceive how the two characters capture a necessary, continued tension in the well-lived life, whether between action and contemplation, theory and practice, work and leisure, or society and solitude.

Where modernity, with its Cartesian lens, insisted that action and contemplation stand in mutually exclusive opposition, we find evidence that we are moving into a new understanding of these terms, along with the world and lives they continue to describe. Far from rendering the ancient debate irrelevant, we find its current version to be drawing closer to ancient and medieval models that held the terms in balance, speaking to the complexities of our world, in which the key categories of work, school, home, and art are under negotiation, while placing new demands on our abilities to interpret the past.

· 1 ·

From Action
and Contemplation to
Stress and Relaxation

The phenomenon of stress among young people is not new, but it appears to be ratcheting up—as is the attention given to it.[1] In our region of northern California, a recent cluster of high school suicides has prompted a new level of urgency, and a determination to understand teenagers' less visible but more pervasive forms of desperation.[2] Parents and schools are beginning to reexamine their approaches, scaling back homework and extracurricular activities and encouraging teens to practice mindfulness meditation and yoga as stress relievers. These responses, however positive, reflect a widely held assumption that stress is a consequence of overscheduling and increased pressure: reduce the pressure and unpack the schedule, it holds, and stress will dissipate. But where this assumption takes the problem to be one of excess—too much homework, pressure, scheduling, distraction—others perceive a larger problem of absence. "The biggest problem growing up today is not actually stress," observes William Damon, professor of education at Stanford. "It's meaninglessness."[3] As Damon argues in his 2008 book *The Path to Purpose*, we could expect more young people to thrive "if, during the early years of strenuous effort and high achievement, they had found purposes that went

deeper than the grades and awards" expected of them.[4] Pur-
poselessness, like stress, he points out, is not confined to the
affluent—those most likely to overschedule their children with
expensive activities and to buy books that tell them not to—but
afflicts all income levels. And, like stress, it requires a remedy
more intensive than relaxation.

Damon's diagnosis of meaninglessness actually returns to
the earliest definitions of "stress." Although it feels like an in-
escapable feature of our age, the term only entered the popular
vocabulary in 1983, when a *Time* magazine cover story declared
"a stress epidemic."[5] Detailing "how heavy a toll stress is taking
on the nation's well being," it found stress to be responsible for
two-thirds of doctor visits in the United States, six of the country's leading causes of death, and untold costs in lost productivity. Hans Selye had first drawn attention to the phenomenon
of "stress" in the 1950s, borrowing from engineering the term
for pressure on an object from an external force. An endocri-
nologist, Selye analyzed in detail the physical manifestations
of stress in the body and advised relaxation as an antidote: "If
we are just doing too much," he observed, "the great remedy
here is to learn to relax as quickly and completely as possible."[6]

Yet even Selye was convinced that the incapacitating stress
he observed in his research subjects and all around him had its
origins and ultimate remedy in the philosophical rather than
the physical realm: the ultimate protection against stress, he
concluded, is "a satisfactory philosophy of life." In *Stress without Distress*, a popular self-help book that he published long
after his research made him famous, Selye elaborated the connection between philosophical and physical health. To remain
healthy, he observed, "man must have some goal, some purpose in life that he can respect and be proud to work for."[7] He
noted that his medical research provided such a purpose—and

a remedy to stress in his own life: "The capacity to contemplate the harmonious elegance of Nature, at least with some degree of understanding, is one of the most satisfactory experiences of which man is capable. . . . There is an equanimity and a peace of mind which can be achieved only through contact with the sublime."[8]

If Selye is the father of modern stress research, the father of modern relaxation research is Harvard cardiologist Herbert Benson, who built on Selye's insights into the physiology of stress. His popular 1975 book, *The Relaxation Response*, recommends the regular practice of deliberate relaxation as "a built-in method of counteracting the stresses of everyday living." Where stress is the by-product of activity, relaxation, according to Benson, involves "the adoption of a passive attitude, which is perhaps the most important of the elements" of its practice.[9] Describing the ancient roots of such relaxation practices in meditation and prayer, he acknowledges that they "may connote exotic Eastern cults or Christian monks who spend most of their waking hours in monastery cells contemplating God." Yet, he insists, even such religious practices hold relevance for modern secular life, a point he makes by citing William James: "To find religion is only one out of many ways of reaching unity; and the process of remedying inner incompleteness and reducing inner discord is a general psychological process."[10]

Much as Selye identifies stress with philosophical failure, Benson identifies relaxation with the healing of psychic, and not merely physiological, wounds: in this, both medical authorities suggest that the work of "reaching unity" and "peace of mind" will ultimately come not from medicine but from a more profound source. Strikingly, the very works that popularized the contemporary sense of "stress" and "relaxation" insist that those terms are inadequate to diagnosing and treating the root problems of the phenomena they describe. Stress, in Selye's account, results not simply from action or overaction but from action unmotivated by a driving purpose. And the need for relaxation, in Benson's view, comes not merely from modern pressures but from a troubling disunity or disharmony at modern humanity's core.

As Selye's and Benson's work has been absorbed into the cultural mainstream, the terms "stress" and "relaxation" have been isolated and treated as purely physiological phenomena; missing are the philosophical disorders that Selye and Benson diagnosed at their base. But without those philosophical underpinnings, stress and relaxation devolve to the therapeutic. They also detach from history, encouraging us to imagine that our contemporary experience is unprecedented. It isn't, of course. But in the absence of historical context or philosophical depth, it resists analysis—and ultimately, understanding.

As used today, "stress" and "relaxation" represent the poor successors to an older and richer pair of terms that can lead us a fuller and deeper understanding of our contemporary struggle. That pair is "action" and "contemplation." Their long and dynamic history embraces meanings that would be at home in our present age—describing, at various times, a life marked by frenetic obligation versus one of deeply centered calm—but it also restores philosophical depth to experiences that we perceive to be historically isolated and isolating. When Benson appeals to the need to "[remedy] inner incompleteness and [reduce] inner discord," he describes a disorder that runs deeper than overscheduling. And when Selye commends "the capacity to contemplate the harmonious elegance of Nature," he imagines no narrowly therapeutic means of stress relief. To restore the significance of these terms—and, by extension, of our current struggle—we will need to turn back to the classical period, where they first took root.

Foundational terms in philosophy and ethics, "contemplation" and "action" represent distinct choices that are fundamental to the well-lived life. They received their earliest definitions in the work of Aristotle and Plato, who use the Greek terms *theoria* and *praxis*, which contrast the philosophical posture of searching and beholding universal meaning with the practical one of acting in the world. For both, "theory" is clearly superior to "practice," but the two cannot be separated. Indeed, they exist in a symbiotic relationship. As Aristotle explains, we pursue action in order to secure time for pure contemplation, just as we fight wars in order to achieve peace. Yet, as Plato insists in his famous model of the philosopher-king, those who achieve the highest states of *theoria* through contemplation are obliged to return to the world and apply their wisdom in its service, no matter how strong their desire to escape it. Neither philosopher could imagine an active life not guided by contemplation, nor a purely contemplative life that did not find expression through action.[11]

But the fortunes of the two terms shifted dramatically once they were taken into other cultures, which adapted them to new circumstances and values. Where the Greeks prized the contemplative life but stressed its integration with action, the ancient Romans emphasized action, scorning the decadence of what they called *otium Graecum*—Greek leisure. Their most eloquent spokesman was the statesman Cicero, who argues that "action is chiefly employed in protecting the interests of our fellow men; it is therefore indispensable to society: and consequently holds a higher rank than mere speculation."[12] Reflecting the ideal of "virtue"—or, as etymology defines it, manly valor—action befits Cicero's Roman republic, which relies on the contributions of its educated citizens. Yet "action" for Cicero is a product of the "liberal" arts, which belong to free men, as opposed to the "servile" arts, the province of mere workers. Cicero's "action" is the work of the brain, not the work of the hands.[13] Opposed to "mere speculation," it is another form of thinking: thinking directed toward the world, not outside it.

The Christian Middle Ages returned to the Greek ideal, preferring contemplation to action, terms adapted to Christian doctrine to elevate the life of prayer over that of worldly commitment and distraction. Still, like the Romans, their greatest spokesmen emphasized the reciprocity of the two. Thus, Saint Augustine sounds like Aristotle when he insists that "no man has a right to lead such a life of contemplation as to forget in his own case the service due to his neighbor; nor has any man a right to be immersed so in active life as to neglect the contemplation of God."[14] Likewise Augustine's follower, theologian Gregory the Great, may hold Plato in mind when he observes that "a good order of life is to strive from the active to the contemplative," but Gregory is also eager to emphasize the interdependence, even the unity, of the two.[15] Just as two eyes working together add dimension to sight, Gregory insists, we must aspire to lives that knit action and contemplation together.[16]

In another vibrant metaphor, Gregory compares the integration of action and contemplation to the unity of breadth and height. So he explains the balanced values of love of neighbor (*vita activa*) and love of God (*vita contemplativa*) along two dimensions: "Breadth pertains to charity for the neighbor; height to the understanding of the Maker. While [the soul] enlarges itself in width through love, it lifts itself in height through knowledge, and it is as high above itself as it extends outside itself in love of neighbor."[17]

Renaissance thinkers recovered Cicero, along with his preference for the active life, even as they expanded the medieval concept of *otium sanctum*—contemplative leisure specific to the life of a monk—to describe the transcendent stillness of the scholar's study. Yet they also inherited the Greek and Christian ideal of a life that embraces and reconciles the two, as Petrarch expresses when he extols the value of "leisure that is neither idle nor profitless but productive of advantage to many."[18] Renaissance education drew from this ideal of contemplative study that could be brought to fruition to benefit the common good.

An important shift in this balance emerges with the advent of the scientific revolution—and with it, a new understanding of "action" as a primary virtue and "contemplation" as not only secondary but debased. The formative work of modern science, Thomas Sprat's *History of the Royal Society* (1667), predicted a new order in which "speculative men" would be ruled by "active men," thanks to advances in science.[19] This view is captured in the title of John Evelyn's *Publick Employment and an Active Life Prefer'd to Solitude* (1667), which asserts that "the most useful and profitable of studies" partake of the active, rather than the contemplative, life: "the *Wisest men* are not made in *chambers* and *Closets* crowded with *shelves*; but by *habitudes* and active *Conversations*." Evelyn could be writing today when he insists that action-driven business trumps contemplation-driven higher education: "Action is the proper fruit of *Science*, and therefore they should quit the education of the *colledge*, when fit to appear in business."[20] Planting science in the camp of action, Evelyn severs it from Augustine's *scientia*, "the intellectual understanding of things eternal," and interrupts a long tradition in which action and contemplation are seen as allied, self-supporting, and even mutually dependent. How do we account for this departure?

Looking back on the period, Hannah Arendt, the greatest modern philosopher of the *vita activa*, explains that the advent of the technological age in the seventeenth century radically disrupted the valuation of action and contemplation that had been in place since the terms' classical origins. In her philosophical masterwork, *The Human Condition* (1958), she asserts that modernity gave priority to action over contemplation to the point of eliminating contemplation as a valuable feature of human life and hollowing out action as the highest expression of human agency. Previously defined as the practice of virtue on behalf of the common good, action came to be identified with "production" and valued as the expression of "productivity." As a result, Arendt argues, the very idea of action lost an important dimension. Instead of carrying intrinsic value, "action" came to mean an undertaking on behalf of some other goal—and thereby became instrumentalized, such that a life of action shed the sense of purpose and dignity that had long defined it. At the same time, wisdom, in the classical sense of the philosophical apprehension of truth, was devalued and superseded by the productive virtues of practicality and utility.[21]

Instrumental thinking is intensely, almost obsessively, oriented toward the future. Once we switch it on, we can't switch it off again. Its depredations are most visible in the lives of the young, like those stress-addled subjects with whom we started. Anxiety around college admissions instrumentalizes school in many communities, where worry and pressure starts by sixth grade and increases through senior year. Among students like those studied by Denise Pope in *Doing School*, school becomes a means to an end. As one teen asserts:

> People don't go to school to learn. They go to get good grades, which brings them to college, which brings them the high-paying job, which brings them happiness, so they think.[22]

Yet once students get to college, the rat race doesn't end. Many college students we know have expressed a growing sense of shock when they discover that the destination they have worked so hard to reach is just another way station on the road to somewhere else. "Getting into Stanford," or any other school, is not an end in itself. The pressure for exemplary grades does not stop. The race for prizes doesn't magically modulate into a life spent conversing about politics, arts, sciences, and pressing issues of the day. Instead, these pressures intensify, even as the path becomes less obvious and economic pressures encroach. Some of our students become quite dismayed when they realize that this pattern extends indefinitely into the future. As the neuroscientist Robert Sapolsky wryly puts it, "We study hard in high school to get admitted to a top college to get into grad school to get a good job to get into the nursing home of our choice."[23]

. . .

Today's "epidemic" of stress and busy-ness represents the far point of the impoverishment of action that Arendt observed: human agency employed in the absence of purpose. Arendt was right to recognize that action began to lose meaning when it was elevated over contemplation, but contemplation was not so starkly eliminated as she believed. Rather, both action and contemplation lost some of the richness of meaning each had, over centuries, been accruing. The polarization of the *vita activa* and the *vita contemplativa* hollowed out the meaning of contemplation no less than it did that of action. If "action" has been reduced to "busy-ness" and its surfeit, "stress," then contemplation has been reduced to "relaxation" and its accompanying, negative attributes—laziness, boredom, and waste of time. Recovering the value both of action and of contemplation means overcoming the polarization that has led to the impoverishment of both terms. This can only happen when we understand that it is the delicate balance of action and contemplation that gives both terms deep significance: action without contemplation becomes meaningless, just as contemplation without action becomes purposeless. Returning each to the other—as writers in earlier ages recognized—restores a balance of action and contemplation in which each is equally necessary to the other, as both are to the maintenance of a meaningful life.

The chapters that follow recover the rich history of action and contemplation, taking up the debate's classic texts, from Aristotle and Aquinas to Bacon and Thoreau, as well as recent writings in the same long tradition. We have been heartened to find that models of the *vita activa* and *vita contemplativa* in dynamic negotiation persist, and in fact are experiencing a resurgence, though often in marginal places and overlooked corners. Part of our aim is to shine a light into these corners in search of the sources of meaning that our culture continually and increasingly seeks.

· 2 ·

The Action Bias and the Human Condition

Two Fantasies

In 1965 Joan Didion wrote a "love song" to John Wayne, an actor who first sauntered into her consciousness when she was a bored eight-year-old child spending a hot dusty summer on an air force base in Colorado. The year was 1943. Wayne's laconic style thrilled her with its easy authority: "'Let's ride,' he said, and 'Saddle up.' 'Forward ho,' and 'A man's gotta do what he's got to do.'" Wayne made everything seem a bit simpler, a bit clearer. "In a world we understood early to be characterized by venality and doubt and polarizing ambiguities, he suggested another world, one which may or may not have existed ever but in any case existed no more; a place where a man could move free, could make his own code and live by it."[1]

Didion was not the only person to fall under his charismatic spell. John Wayne mesmerized American culture. As the moving parts of the political world grew ever more unwieldy, Wayne came to symbolize a past where causes and effects were easier to grasp. He helped people believe in a sharp and obvious difference between action and muddle, doing and navel-gazing, right and wrong. Although his support of the Vietnam War became well known, John Wayne never ran for political office. But others like him certainly have. Hollywood's most famous Republican officeholders have based their political personas on action heroes and, indeed, cowboys: Clint Eastwood, Ronald Reagan, Arnold Schwarzenegger. They promise to ride into town and restore the bright line that has been lost under mudslides of process and bureaucracy. The cowboy politician asks neither permission nor forgiveness. He promises to act, to get it done.

The story is by now very familiar. The cowboy politician rides past in a flash of color. He stands for something real against the bland, soulless technocrats. We live in a world gone mad with political correctness and proceduralism, run by timid bureaucrats who jealously guard their own power. The fantasy is that somebody decisive will come along and, well, do something.

The fantasy is that a well-placed thunderbolt can solve our problems. Why can't we just cut through the red tape, cut off consultation and deliberation, and unfetter ourselves from the proceduralists? George Bush and Dick Cheney rode this fantasy to power in 2000. Having followed political advice never to compromise, Bush repeatedly said that life would be simpler if he could be a dictator. By one standard account, Cheney was so maddened by the flaccidity of the executive branch in the 1970s that he sought to make it manly again.[2]

The story is a staple of police dramas. Stymied by his process-loving bosses, the heroic cop relies on his own street smarts to solve crimes, fighting both the criminals and the dunderheaded bureaucrats who tell him to back off. Dirty Harry Callahan, Eastwood's iconic San Francisco police officer, was an early avatar. In our political culture, action is celebrated and lionized—no public voices question its power. To hear any politician or pundit tell it, action is a heroic battle against sclerotic, obstructionist forces. Sports and military metaphors abound in depictions of action as the armor, breastplate, shield, and arrow of the righteous warrior.

Yet this fantasy hides from us a darker truth, namely that action is hard to do and even harder to do well. Actions swerve unpredictably off their tracks. "Heroism is bravery and selflessness, but more than that, it is triumphant action, and in particular, morally unambiguous action," writes William Deresiewicz. But, he reminds us:

> In most of life—and certainly in public life—there is scarcely such a thing on either count. Politics is a muddle of moral and practical compromise. Victories are almost always partial, ambiguous and subject to reversal. Heroism belongs to the realm of fantasy—the comic book, the action movie— or to delimited and often artificial spheres of action, like space exploration or sports.[3]

He is right. In a multipolar world, politics are built on shifting sands where solutions are temporary and incremental. Cowboy politicians are just as likely as other politicians to have their actions thwarted, reversed, criticized, scrutinized, undone.

Our business culture fantasizes about action as well. Its vocabulary is blunt: impact, motivation, plan, power, productivity, agenda, action item, energy, strategic dynamism. The words race to conclusions. A Chicago hedge-fund manager confidently told one of us before the Iraq war was launched that the conflict was already "done, baked." These are trader's term to describe an action whose outcome is so certain as to seem already to have happened.

One of the best-selling business books of all time—*In Search of Excellence* by Tom Peters and Robert Waterman—hammers home the point that successful companies have a bias toward action. Great companies get things done. They do not overanalyze problems but gear their teams to cut through layers of bureaucratic obstruction and get results. Yet the more business writers exhort people to action, the stronger the layers of bureaucratic obstruction seem to grow. *In Search of Excellence* was first published in the 1980s. Even then, Peters and Waterman railed against a corporate culture of paper pushing:

> Most of the institutions that we spend time with are ensnared in massive reports that have been massaged by various staffs and sometimes, quite literally, hundreds of staffers. All the life is pressed out of the ideas; only an iota of personal accountability remains. Big companies seem to foster huge laboratory operations that produce papers and patents by the ton, but rarely new products. These companies are besieged by vast interlocking sets of committees and task forces that drive out creativity and block action. Work is governed by an absence of realism, spawned by staffs of people who haven't made or sold, tried, tasted, or sometimes even seen the product, but instead, have learned about it from reading dry reports produced by other staffers.[4]

Setting institutional productivity apart from institutional reflection—the reports and laboratories that form the contemplative arms of industry—Peters and Waterman proffer an attractive fantasy of unfettered action. A rich vein of satire has ridiculed the business world's obsession with process, highlighting the pointless busy-ness and paper shuffling that often passes for work. The business bureaucracy, this satire tells us, mimics the language of action (outcomes assessments, results orientation, and so on) mainly in order to perpetuate its own machinery.

To distill a few drops wof action out of sludgy rivers of process, Silicon Valley companies innovate like mad. Stand-up meetings seem to work well, yet they are newsworthy not be-

FIGURE 1. Scott Adams, "Our new philosophy is 'a bias for action.'"
From *Dilbert* © 2007 Scott Adams. Used by permission
of Universal Uclick. All rights reserved.

cause they are so common but because they are so rare. A vast
consulting industry promises to help people focus, be more productive, and—as a popular book and its associated suite of productivity tools has it—Get Things Done. But when one reads
all this zealous, hortatory literature, one gets the sense that the
productivity industry thrives on the same diet of perpetual failure as the happiness industry does. If people could achieve happiness by way of a formula, the industry would immediately col-
lapse. Likewise, if a bias for action and frictionless productivity
could be inculcated by a single management guru, there would
be no such guru in the first place.

． ． ．

For many decades, American business culture has been singing
a leftish version of this love song too, though as a minor chord
within the dominant key. Sung in the style of Thoreau by young
idealists and satirists (as Thoreau himself was), this love song
is also about action. It goes like this: The modern world is intensely alienating. Corporate culture is dehumanizing and abstract. Your career will consists of shuffling paper in a cubicle

as you specialize and narrow, narrow and specialize, becoming little more than a faceless cog in a joyless machine.

This vision of soulless work is almost as old as American business itself. In *Bartleby the Scrivener*, a story written in 1853, Herman Melville paints a picture of office work as pointless busy-ness. In one passage the narrator, a man who runs an office of copyists, describes the empty but noisy work habits of one of his employees: "He made an unpleasant racket with his chair; spilled his sand-box; in mending his pens, impatiently split them all to pieces, and threw them on the floor in a sudden passion; stood up and leaned over his table, boxing his papers about in a most indecorous manner, very sad to behold in an elderly man like him." "Nevertheless" he adds, "he was in many ways a most valuable person to me."

For the young person of grand ideals, a future pushing paper is a living death. His or her passions, whatever they once were, wither on the vine. To salvage a few molecules of humanity, the young idealist must push back against this massive, alienating system and find a way back to the things he or she cares about. Often these fantasies involve making things by hand, a sort of labor that has been devalued in the past century. Surely if we just found our way back to a simpler greener world, our minds, freed from doubt and angst, would stop racing.

This story, too, is almost as old as American culture. "Why," Thoreau asks, should people "begin digging their graves as soon as they are born?" *Walden* brims with contempt for the "mean and sneaking lives" most people live, "lying, flattering, voting, contracting yourselves into a nutshell of civility or dilating into an atmosphere of thin and vaporous generosity." Thoreau thinks his readers debase themselves just so "that you may persuade your neighbor to let you make his shoes, or his hat, or his coat, or his carriage, or import his groceries for him;

making yourselves sick, that you may lay up something against a sick day."[5] He and Emerson and their Concord circle imagined that people could escape the money-mad world, a world in which language had become as debased as any paper currency, and create a world by the work of their own hands.

Having gotten a PhD in political philosophy from the University of Chicago, Matthew Crawford started working at a think tank in Washington. But, he writes, "I was always tired, and honestly could not see the rationale for my being paid at all—what tangible goods or useful services was I providing to anyone? This sense of uselessness was dispiriting. The pay was good, but it truly felt like compensation, and after five months I quit to open the bike shop." Crawford turned to fixing motorcycle engines, a job as tough and intellectually subtle as the philosophizing he had been doing, but one where he felt actual outcomes were at stake. He writes movingly of leaving behind "the world of work, where the experience of individual agency has become elusive. Those who work in an office often feel that, despite the proliferation of contrived metrics they must meet, their job lacks objective standards of the sort provided by, for example, a carpenter's level."[6] And he indicts the sort of work a college graduate might now look forward to finding:

> Managers themselves inhabit a bewildering psychic landscape, and are made anxious by the vague imperatives they must answer to. The college student interviews for a job as a knowledge worker, and finds that the corporate recruiter never asks him about his grades and doesn't care what he majored in. He senses that what is demanded of him is not knowledge but rather that he project a certain kind of personality, an affable complaisance. Is all his hard work in school somehow just for show—his ticket to a Potemkin

meritocracy? There seems to be a mismatch between form and content, and a growing sense that the official story we've been telling ourselves about work is somehow false.[7]

A job as a "knowledge worker" is what many stressed-out high school students aspire to—but what, Crawford implies, does the epithet really mean? Is it more than a fancy job title—a bit of linguistic inflation?

The transcendentalists worried about inflation too. Emerson wondered how we could reawaken our souls in a world in which language had grown so shallow. He likens this dead language to paper money that has gone off the gold standard, a debased and inflationary currency, a "fraud":

> In due time, the fraud is manifest, and words lose all power to stimulate the understanding or the affections. But wise men pierce this rotten diction and fasten words again to visible things.[8]

How do we do this? We reignite the passion of language, putting it back into contact with nature—or in Crawford's telling, putting ourselves back into contact with actual, physical work.

. . .

Both of these cultural narratives—the cowboy and the nonconformist—carry political associations: the cowboy tends toward right-wing politics, the nonconformist, left-wing. Yet they have much in common. Both stories imagine that modern people grope around in an alien fog, having suffered what T. S. Eliot called a "dissociation of sensibilities." The practical and the meaningful parts of life have split apart. To connect them again, we make an uneasy bargain. On the one hand, contemplation is presented as a luxury nobody can afford to pursue. On the other, consumer culture expresses a deep nostalgia for a simpler, more contemplative life. Vacation experts, style gurus, and interior designers aggressively package fantasies of living a slow, stress-free life suffused with simple beauty, perhaps in a Tuscan monastery repurposed as a boutique hotel.[9] Marketing aside, people have responded creatively to what they feel as a lack, experimenting with ways to resist the ever-quickening pace of life. But, as Crawford observes:

> The mortgage broker works hard all year, then he goes and climbs Mount Everest. The exaggerated psychic content of his summer vacation sustains him through the fall, winter, and spring. . . . There is a disconnect between his work life and his leisure life; in the one he accumulates money and in the other he accumulates psychic nourishment. Each part depends on and enables the other, but does so in the manner of a transaction between sub-selves, rather than as the intelligibly linked parts of a coherent life.[10]

In this book, we are looking for alternatives to the contemporary story about the contemplative life, pursuing ways of thinking that integrate action and contemplation rather than pitting them against each other. Crawford seeks one form of this integration in his vision of "soulcraft." Another vision belongs largely to the German philosopher Hannah Arendt, though other thinkers (including Emerson) have expressed some version of it too. The dream is less an intellectual tradition than a critique. It can serve as a compass or mental corrective to our compulsive culture. Its most appealing element is that it does not advocate any action at all—neither dropping out (like Thoreau) nor taking down the rotten edifice (like John Wayne).

Arendt believed that modern cultures push us into a narrowly practical and technocratic way of thinking. Instrumental reason—the sort of means-end thinking that chooses relentlessly from a limited set of goals—has its place in our lives, but when we give ourselves over to it, it becomes a taskmaster we try desperately to please despite the risk to our souls. When we try to measure our lives instrumentally, we fail to recognize a simple truth: the meaning of actions comes from the stories we tell. Stories are like a gong whose sounds echo far and wide. We can plan our actions but cannot control how they turn out or, indeed, how other people will make sense of them.

Students often say they want to have an impact. Of course they mean that they want to have a positive impact. But how easy is it to anticipate what impact our actions may have? Bad consequences are just as likely as good ones. So are mixed and incoherent results. Action is less a matter of cause and effect than a process of history unfolding unpredictably. As Emerson wrote in his great visionary essay *Experience*, hoping to ease his suffering after his five-year-old son died:

> The results of life are uncalculated and uncalculable. The years teach much which the days never know. The persons who compose our company, converse, and come and go, and design and execute many things, and somewhat comes of it all, but an unlooked-for result. The individual is always mistaken. He designed many things, and drew in other persons as coadjutors, quarreled with some or all, blundered much, and something is done; all are a little advanced, but the individual is always mistaken. It turns out somewhat new, and very unlike what he promised himself.[11]

Emerson's words, written in 1844, almost perfectly foreshadow those of Arendt as she muses on the ancient concept of the active life in the wake of the Second World War. Arendt wanted to restore a lost ideal of openness to the world, in response to what she saw as the clenching of the modern spirit. Arendt understood that humans live in webs of stories, of meaning, of feeling, but that modern people lose contact with this web of meaning through ever-increasing attention to efficiency and control, specifically control over nature through technical processes.

Arendt's terms may seem counterintuitive, especially in our present dilemma. We work all the time, yet it is work that prevents us from acting. Work is instrumental, short-term, and outcome-oriented. Action, on the other hand, is fundamentally social and life-affirming. By action, Arendt does not mean what John Wayne (much less Dilbert's boss) means. She means not the pursuit of outcomes through technique or control, but rather the initiation of actions in the absence of objectives. Action, in her understanding, is among the highest ideals of human life and consists in stories whose outcomes are known only much later: "Action reveals itself fully only to the storyteller, that is, to the backward glance of the historian, who indeed always knows better what it was all about than the participants."[12]

In *The Human Condition*, Arendt calls action "the one miracle-working faculty of man" and "the miracle which saves the world." "Only the full experience of this capacity can bestow upon human affairs faith and hope."[13] Emerson, too, uses "miracle" to denote a force that cannot be captured by a narrow set of instruments:

> The ancients, struck with this irreducibleness of the elements of human life to calculation, exalted Chance into a divinity, but that is to stay too long at the spark,—which glitters truly at one point,—but the universe is warm with the

latency of the same fire. The miracle of life which will not be expounded, but will remain a miracle, introduces a new element.[14]

"The miracle of life which will not be expounded"; "the miracle which saves the world"—Emerson's and Arendt's words about action are electrifying. Both were fascinated, indeed filled with awe, by the surprising shapes our lives and stories take.

The Human Condition is mainly a polemic. Arendt's ideas are subtle and not entirely predictable. Although she is a philosopher, she does not argue that her lost ideal of action can be found in the contemplative life or in philosophy. A Jewish refugee from Nazi Germany, she found her way to New York, where she taught at the New School for Social Research and wrote books of political theory. She pondered the roots of totalitarianism. In 1951 she wrote extensively about racism, imperialism, and colonialism. In 1958, when she wrote *The Human Condition*, her target was larger: nothing less than the strands of political philosophy that had led people to overvalue their sense of control and technical mastery over the ever-unpredictable forces in life.

Arendt thought that modern life had degraded the ancient ideal of the active life into something meager—a mere hunt for efficiency. Moderns turn the world into numbers, not words, hewing to a tragically narrow rationality. The "typical attitude" of modern man includes

> his instrumentalization of the world, his confidence in tools and in the productivity of the maker of artificial objects; his trust in the all-comprehensive range of the means-end category, his conviction that every issue can be solved and every human motivation reduced to the principle of utility; his sovereignty, which regards everything given as material

and thinks of the whole of nature as of "an immense fabric from which we can cut out whatever we want to resew it however we like"; his equation of intelligence with ingenuity, that is, his contempt for all thought which cannot be considered to be "the first step . . . for the fabrication of artificial objects, particularly of tools to make tools, and to vary their fabrication indefinitely"; finally, his matter-of-course identification of fabrication with action.[15]

Arendt found this modern vision both limiting and dangerous. But her target is not only the modern work obsessive or efficiency addict (a type she calls "*homo faber*," or fabricating man). *Homo faber* is a symptom of a broader problem.

Modern life rests on a mistaken and dangerous fantasy of control. Arendt had become convinced that certain strains of philosophy arose from just such a fantasy—specifically the fantasy of standing outside history and directing its outcomes. Philosophy contradicts the human condition. The word "condition" is worth pausing over.[16] To be "conditioned" is to recognize our own contingency, frailty, particularity. To be conditioned is to be modest and tactful, to recognize that we depend upon each other and upon our circumstances: "life itself, natality, mortality, worldliness, plurality, and the earth."[17] Any mode of life that severs thought from action estranges human beings from our awareness of how we are grounded in the human condition.

Philosophy's basic error, for which Arendt blames Plato, was to think itself unconditioned, independent, abstracted, set apart. Plato's philosophy begins with "the shocked wonder at the miracle of Being." This shocked wonder stems from "an experience, perhaps the most striking one, that Socrates offered his disciples: the sight of him time and again suddenly overcome by his thoughts and thrown into a state of absorption to the point of motionlessness for many hours." Philosophy, thus founded, severed the intellectual life from "the work of our hands."[18]

Philosophy's desire for ecstasy—for standing apart—led at best to quiet self-absorption and at worst to love of tyrants. After the Second World War, Arendt saw philosophy in the darkest possible light. By standing mutely outside the political sphere, she thought, philosophers had been guilty of tacitly endorsing National Socialism. Of course, some philosophers had not stood mutely outside. Her teacher, friend, and former lover Martin Heidegger had apparently enthusiastically joined the Nazi party. (Although Heidegger himself was an anti-Platonist, believing not in mystical forms beyond the here and now but in our thorough immersion in the stuff of the world, he had apparently committed Plato's mistake in overvaluing thought.)[19]

Years later, Arendt seemed to have forgiven him. Writing on his eightieth birthday, she likened Heidegger to the ancient Thracian philosopher Thales who, while staring intently at the sky, fell into a ditch. A milkmaid laughed at him for being too stupid to see what was under his feet. (For a philosopher, to be laughed at is surely more humiliating than to be refuted.) Heidegger is Thales and, by implication, Arendt is the milkmaid. All philosophers fall down, like Thales, when they step into public life, Arendt argues. When they do enter politics, they gravitate toward tyrants, a fact she finds "striking and perhaps exasperating" but attributes less to personal failing than to a "deformation professionelle." In the end, she absolves, Heidegger, releasing him from ordinary history and time. For these philosophers,

> it does not finally matter where the storms of their century may have driven them. For the wind that blows through Heidegger's thinking—like that which still sweeps toward

us after thousands of years from the work of Plato—does not spring from the century he happens to live in. It comes from the primeval, and what it leaves behind is something perfect, something which, like everything perfect (in Rilke's words), falls back to where it came from.[20]

Arendt's hostility to philosophy—and through philosophy, to the *vita contemplativa*—arises from profound disgust with a tradition she had avidly studied as a young woman.[21] She is also an arch-pessimist: when she paints the modern world, her palette ranges from mood indigo to inky black. Her pessimism may have blinded her to capitalism's many benefits. Yet she was obviously right about other aspects of modern society. She foresaw strains in the culture that would only grow more potent over time. So let us step back from Arendt for a moment and look with a wider lens at the fantasy of control that she deemed so central to modern life.

The Fantasy of Control

Let's start with our love affair with data. "To count is a modern practice, the ancient method was to guess," wrote Samuel Johnson in 1775.[22] Even Johnson, though, would have been shocked at how completely numbers now rule our lives. To King Lear's searing question "Who is it that can tell me who I am?" fast-flowing data streams pump out answers. The "data-driven life" has caromed past "the purpose-driven life." Gary Wolf, a journalist who covers the growing practice of self-tracking, started a website called *Quantified Self*:

> We began holding regular meetings for people running interesting personal data projects. I had recently written a

long article about a trend among Silicon Valley types who time their days in increments as small as two minutes, and I suspected that the self-tracking explosion was simply the logical outcome of this obsession with efficiency. We use numbers when we want to tune up a car, analyze a chemical reaction, predict the outcome of an election. We use numbers to optimize an assembly line. Why not use numbers on ourselves?

Why not indeed? If "man is a machine," as the eighteenth-century French writer La Mettrie asserted, then man can be infinitely tuned up. Except what do tracking statistics really show? Wolf's website brims with applications, discussion forums, and every technology imaginable to help people track microscopic details of their lives. The quantified self has replaced the language-based self:

> Ubiquitous self-tracking is a dream of engineers. For all their expertise at figuring out how things work, technical people are often painfully aware how much of human behavior is a mystery. People do things for unfathomable reasons. They are opaque even to themselves. A hundred years ago, a bold researcher fascinated by the riddle of human personality might have grabbed onto new psychoanalytic concepts like repression and the unconscious. These ideas were invented by people who loved language. Even as therapeutic concepts of the self spread widely in simplified, easily accessible form, they retained something of the prolix, literary humanism of their inventors. From the languor of the analyst's couch to the chatty inquisitiveness of a self-help questionnaire, the dominant forms of self-exploration assume that the road to knowledge lies through words. Trackers are exploring an alternate route. Instead of

interrogating their inner worlds through talking and writing, they are using numbers.

Recently, Wolf writes, he has noticed something like mission creep among the self-trackers. Self-tracking can help people change their habits: researchers concluded years ago that people act differently in response to being measured, dubbing the phenomenon the Hawthorne effect. But now data has rapidly morphed from a tool to an end in itself:

> I soon realized that an emphasis on efficiency missed something important. Efficiency implies rapid progress toward a known goal. For many self-trackers, the goal is unknown. Although they may take up tracking with a specific question in mind, they continue because they believe their numbers hold secrets that they can't afford to ignore, including answers to questions they have not yet thought to ask.[23]

Language may leave our self-conceptions shrouded in mystery, but do numbers fare any better in telling us who we are? In 1798 William Wordsworth, a writer who feared the rise of scientific instrumentality, cried out, "Our meddling intellect / Mis-shapes the beauteous forms of things:—We murder to dissect." But perhaps Wordsworth need not have feared. The data revolution does not seem to have murdered our souls with a dissecting scalpel so much as slathered them in statistics. And statistics, as people have known at least since Disraeli's famous line about "lies, damned lies and statistics," can be massaged, cherry-picked, and manipulated. (*How to Lie with Statistics* was the title of a famous book from 1954.)

The deeper truth is that people use statistics to tell stories. Our stories hang around our shoulders like cloaks: we sincerely believe that we have chosen their cut and color for ourselves, but these features fashion our beliefs as much as our beliefs fashion them. We swaddle ourselves in these cloaks believing we have chosen our own fit. But the modern world shapes our perceptions into patterns, making available certain kinds of stories on which we model our lives. In the social sciences this phenomenon is called a "looping effect." New categories beget the thing categorized, concepts beget the thing conceptualized, stories beget the characters in those stories.

Looping effects can be enormously powerful. Consider the fact, well documented by the San Francisco writer Ethan Watters, that the American psychiatric establishment has effectively exported American-style mental illnesses to other cultures by supplying them with diagnostic categories:

> The American Psychiatric Association's *Diagnostic and Statistical Manual of Mental Disorders*, the *DSM* (the "bible" of the profession, as it is sometimes called), has become the worldwide standard. In addition, American researchers and organizations run the premier scholarly journals and host top conferences in the fields of psychology and psychiatry. Western universities train the world's most influential clinicians and academics. Western drug companies dole out the funds for research and spend billions marketing medications for mental illnesses. Western-trained traumatologists rush in wherever war or natural disasters strike to deliver "psychological first aid," bringing with them their assumptions about how the mind becomes broken and how it is best healed.[24]

Suddenly rates of anorexia, depression, schizophrenia, and PTSD have spiked in places like China, Japan, and Sri Lanka where they had been rare if not unheard of until recently. Perhaps these diseases were underreported and new diagnostic tools make it easier for doctors to spot them? No. Watters argues persuasively that diagnostic categories create the very diseases they purport to diagnose.

This sort of thing is not supposed to happen in the age of neuroscience. Objective measures are supposed to correct for cultural variance. But the truth is, the stories we tell about mental states alter our experience of our own mental state:

> We can become psychologically unhinged for many reasons, such as personal trauma, social upheaval, or a chemical imbalance in our brain. Whatever the cause, we invariably rely on cultural beliefs and stories to understand what is happening. Those stories, whether they tell of spirit possession or serotonin depletion, shape the experience of the illness in surprisingly dramatic and often counterintuitive ways.[25]

Mental states are like gas molecules. They shape themselves to whatever containers they are in. And stories are those containers.

Homo faber, to use Arendt's term, has been one of the most powerful avatars in and for the Western psyche since at least the seventeenth century. *Homo faber* is the lone individual busily and heroically turning things around him to some practical use. *Robinson Crusoe*, a novel published in 1719, has long been seen as the story of economic man. Washed up on an uninhabited island, Crusoe spends nearly thirty years building a fortress for himself. He leaves a society dominated by laws, regulations, and governments, and slowly, surely builds the whole thing up again from scratch. Eventually he becomes the totalitarian governor of a small state marked by hierarchy, subordination, and division of labor. He obsessively calculates use-value, constantly fitting things to ends. He gradually encloses the land and animals he finds. He expands his circle, arming himself and extending his mastery over new zones and sectors. His stance is reduced to a crouch, and he repeatedly offers such self-observations as, "I put myself into all the same Postures for an Attack, that I had formerly provided, and was just ready for Action, if any thing had presented."

Looping effects, however, can push this elemental story—call it the story of the libertarian self—in a monstrous direction. Film and video have propelled into global consciousness a powerful avatar: a lone shooter armed to the teeth facing off against seas of enemies. First-person shooter video games are full of mayhem and have spurred heated debate about the degree to which they contribute to real-world violence. In the decade following the 1999 mass killing at Columbine High School in Colorado, controversy bubbled in the media and courts about such video games. The two Columbine killers, had become experts at *Doom*, a game in which players take on the point of view of a US Marine assailed by hostile Martians. The marine is represented onscreen by an array of weapons. More recently, the Norwegian white supremacist who killed seventy-seven people, mostly teenagers, in the summer of 2011, told the court that he used the game *Call of Duty: Modern Warfare* as a training simulator, claiming armies all over the world use the game to hone marksmanship skills.[26] In 2001 some families of the Columbine victims sued Id software and other game makers, alleging, among other things, that the games teach people to fire weapons without teaching them to handle them safely (the lawsuit was dismissed). Gamers have fought back vigorously against the media-driven storyline that has them turning into mindless, "zombified addicts."[27]

Here is a terrible paradox. The less certain we find ourselves, the more we crave certainty and control. And the more we crave certainty, the more we try to take matters into our own hands.

Take the example of elite soccer goalkeepers. Most soccer fans dread penalty shootouts, used to break ties, often in important games with vast amounts of money and prestige at stake. The opposing goalkeepers each face a series of kickers, and are most often humiliated. The kicker stands thirty-six feet away and fires the ball at speeds up to eighty miles an hour toward a net twenty-four feet wide. The goalkeeper has only two-tenths of a second to work out what to do and usually has to commit before the kick is launched. But even with these many advantages, kickers sometimes miss or have their shots blocked. When that happens, the shame can linger for decades. To save everybody a great deal of pain, the referee should probably just let the match be decided by a coin toss.

But games are not rational, however much we may wish they were, because players are not rational. They often fail, as economists delicately put it, to maximize their own utility. In 2007 a team of Israeli behavioral economists published a paper about how elite goalkeepers defend against penalty kicks. Goalkeepers, they show, are often their own worst enemies. They make a difficult task even harder by trying to do something—anything—to solve it. The economists' findings were written up in the business section of the *New York Times*:

> For their study, Mr. Azar, along with Michael Bar-Eli, a sports psychologist; Ilana Ritov, a psychologist; and two graduate students, scanned the top leagues in the world, collecting data on 311 penalty kicks. Then they computed the probability of stopping different kicks (to the left, the right or center) with different actions (jumping left, right, or staying put) to see which one "maximizes his chance of stopping the ball." According to their calculations, staying in the center gives the goalkeeper the best shot at halting a penalty kick—33.3 percent, instead of 14.2 percent on the

left and 12.6 percent on the right. Yet when the group analyzed how the goalkeepers had actually reacted to these
penalty kicks, they discovered the goalies remained in the
center just 6.3 percent of the time.[28]

Goalkeepers obviously want to stop penalty kicks. Yet they act
in a way that makes them less likely to do so. Why? When asked,
most goalies reported feeling worse about missing penalty kicks
when they just stood still than when they lunged to the side. If
they were going to fail, better to go down doing something than
standing still and looking weak. Yet they end up worse off than
if they had done nothing.

Social scientists have called this feeling "action bias." We
will examine the action part of it in a moment, but first a word or
two on the term "bias," which means something specific. Compared to computers, humans are notoriously bad at reasoning.
We often take quick and easy mental shortcuts—and not just
quick and easy, but false: our mental shortcuts tend to be self-
serving and overly optimistic. These shortcuts are called cognitive biases and they can be very hard to correct. The system-
atic study of cognitive biases began in Israel in the 1960s, when
two young researchers, Daniel Kahnemann and Amos Tversky, started asking questions about how people reason. Their
research program has yielded enormous fruit: they invented a
new academic field, turned out new research agendas across
the social sciences, and Kahnemann garnered a Nobel Prize in
economics (Tversky having died some years before). In an autobiography posted on the Nobel website, Kahneman recalls the
insight that led him to develop his new field:

I had the most satisfying Eureka experience of my career
while attempting to teach flight instructors that praise

is more effective than punishment for promoting skill-
learning. When I had finished my enthusiastic speech, one
of the most seasoned instructors in the audience raised
his hand and made his own short speech, which began by
conceding that positive reinforcement might be good for
the birds, but went on to deny that it was optimal for flight
cadets. He said, "On many occasions I have praised flight
cadets for clean execution of some aerobatic maneuver,
and in general when they try it again, they do worse. On
the other hand, I have often screamed at cadets for bad
execution, and in general they do better the next time. So
please don't tell us that reinforcement works and punishment does not, because the opposite is the case." This was
a joyous moment, in which I understood an important truth
about the world: because we tend to reward others when
they do well and punish them when they do badly, and because there is regression to the mean, it is part of the human
condition that we are statistically punished for rewarding
others and rewarded for punishing them. I immediately ar-
ranged a demonstration in which each participant tossed
two coins at a target behind his back, without any feedback.
We measured the distances from the target and could see
that those who had done best the first time had mostly de-
teriorated on their second try, and vice versa. But I knew
that this demonstration would not undo the effects of lifelong exposure to a perverse contingency.

Kahneman had found out something important about how
people think. The flight instructor noticed certain patterns.
Flight cadets generally did worse on a task after they were
praised. When they were yelled at, they generally did better. So
he told Kahneman he was wrong to think praise is the key to

learning: in his experience, punishment was far more reliable. But Kahneman realized that the instructor was wrong—and wrong because he was in the grip of an illusion that he could not see past. Whenever the cadets performed especially badly or especially well, their performance was most likely a quirk, an outlier. On the next maneuver, the student was bound to fall closer to his own average, even if his skills were slowly improving over time. Praise or punishment actually had little effect on how well a student did—his performance would have "regress[ed] to the mean" no matter what. The flight instructor nonetheless (logically) assumed that his own actions were responsible for how his students performed. He could see that when he acted on a student, the student responded, so he assumed that his actions caused the student to respond.

This illusion, Kahneman notes, encourages an unfounded belief: because we see people getting better after we punish them and getting worse after we praise them, we conclude that punishment is more effective. *Sports Illustrated* has long been the subject of just such an illusion, the widespread belief among athletes that appearing on the magazine's cover spells doom (the "curse" of *Sports Illustrated*). In fact, many athletes asked to appear on the cover have been on hot streaks that would cool off anyway. The cover just happens to mark the peak of their success.[29]

In studying the way people make decisions, Kahneman and Tversky turned up a host of findings about how people reason. For example, we hate losing money, so much so that we prefer to risk a large loss if there is even a small chance we will lose no money to accepting a sure loss of a smaller amount. Thus we make financial decisions that look ridiculous in hindsight. Nick Leeson, the "rogue trader" who in 1995 brought down Barings, a bank founded in 1762, claimed that his bad trades started when a trading mistake by one of his colleagues resulted in a loss of twenty thousand pounds. He hid the loss and tried to make up for it with increasingly speculative trades. In the end he lost 827 million pounds, and Barings went bankrupt. Such anecdotes make it hard to depict humans as rational decision makers.

While irrational financial behavior is serious enough, some of our biases are truly alarming. In 2006 Kahneman and Jonathan Renshon, a doctoral student at Harvard, published a slight essay with a profound message: most of our cognitive biases favor the hawkish side of our nature rather than the dovish. These biases can lead to a persistent "policy capture" favoring war over peace. They "incline national leaders to exaggerate the evil intentions of adversaries, to misjudge how adversaries perceive them, to be overly sanguine when hostilities start, and overly reluctant to make necessary concessions in negotiations. In short, these biases have the effect of making wars more likely to begin and more difficult to end."

These biases include the "fundamental attribution error"— the mistake of thinking that because somebody advocates a position, the position comes from some essential place deep inside them, rather than from the usual mix of local circumstances that we ourselves are aware of:

> Imagine, for example, that you have been placed in a room and asked to watch a series of student speeches on the policies of Venezuelan leader Hugo Chávez. You've been told in advance that the students were assigned the task of either attacking or supporting Chávez and had no choice in the matter. Now, suppose that you are then asked to assess the political leanings of these students. Shrewd observers, of course, would factor in the context and adjust

their assessments accordingly. A student who gave an enthusiastic pro-Chávez speech was merely doing what she was told, not revealing anything about her true attitudes. In fact, many experiments suggest that people would overwhelmingly rate the pro-Chávez speakers as more leftist. Even when alerted to context that should affect their judgment, people tend to ignore it. Instead, they attribute the behavior they see to the person's nature, character, or persistent motives.[30]

So we hold other people to their opinions, imagining that those opinions reflect some deep identity.

One bias stands out above the rest, and indeed explains why many other biases are so common: the illusion of control. First identified by Ellen Langer in 1975, it is the tendency, as she put it somewhat drily, to "assume a skill orientation in chance situations."[31] In a casino, people behave as though furrowing their brows, blowing into their hands, or throwing extra hard or soft will make the dice roll go their way.[32] In sports, the illusion of control leads to some funny rituals. Pitchers often go through an elaborate set routine before pitching, pinching the resin bag, running their toe just-so over the pitching rubber, touching parts of their uniform in sequence. Wade Boggs, the great Red Sox third baseman, ate chicken before every game. Whole websites chronicle the quirks and superstitions of professional athletes (Serena Williams is said to wear the same pair of socks throughout a tournament). Anthropologist Bruno Malinowski discovered that "tribes of the Trobriand islands who fish in the deep sea, where sudden storms and unmapped waters are constant concerns, have far more rituals associated with fishing than do those who fish in shallow waters."[33]

The less control we have in a situation, the more likely we

are to find patterns in the world around us. The illusion of control is a way of imposing order on chaos. Such, at any rate, was the finding of a series of studies done by two researchers at the University of Texas and Northwestern University in 2008. Participants were given random feedback on a task and then asked to find patterns in pictures from which computers had "eliminate[d] any trace of the embedded image."[34] The less control people had over their performance on the task the more likely they were to see patterns where none existed. They were also more likely to find conspiracies in stories and, when told that the stock market was volatile, to overestimate the amount of negative information available about a fictional company.[35] As the researchers put it, "Experiencing a loss of control led participants to desire more structure and to perceive illusory patterns. The need to be and feel in control is so strong that individuals will produce a pattern from noise to return the world to a predictable state."[36] Even exposure to absurdist art can have the same effect: one study found that "participants who were exposed to absurdist art or reminders of their mortality"—in the form of stories by Kafka and Monty Python—"reported higher scores on the Personal Need for Structure scale, suggesting that they experienced a heightened need for meaning."[37]

Pattern seeking and ritual behavior seem harmless enough—even if they are triggered only by the story of a giant cockroach or a skit about a dead parrot. However, the illusion of control can feed intuitions so strong that their grip is devilishly hard to break. Most people feel safe if they are directly in control, yet it is much safer to fly on a jet piloted by somebody else than it is to drive a car. Car makers and the gun lobby have notoriously exploited this (false) intuition to our detriment. Many people keep guns at home because they feel guns protect their families from intruders. But the reverse is true: bringing a gun into the house is the fastest way to put a family at risk. Rates of suicide, homicide, and accidental deaths spike dramatically. "If you bought a gun today, I could tell you the risk of suicide to you and your family members is going to be two- to tenfold higher over the next twenty years," Matthew Miller, a Harvard epidemiologist, told journalist Shankar Vedantam. "There are not many things you can do to increase your risk of dying tenfold."[38] So too with SUV ownership in the 1990s. Advertisements relentlessly stoked the idea we were most threatened by other drivers and by foul weather—hostile forces outside ourselves. People could thus ignore data about rollover risks. Because people feel safest having their hands on the steering wheel (or their finger on the trigger), stories that confirm such biases tend to spread more easily than stories that contradict them.

The Action Bias and the Human Condition

Modern market society and corporate capitalism strongly encourage utilitarian calculation and demand technocratic efficiency. They ask us to treat other people as means to an end rather than as ends in themselves. Obviously, these conditions raise many questions: Is this way of living good for our souls? How can we fashion selves—selves that we admire and can live with—when we are asked to treat other people (and ourselves) as instruments? And finally, how much of this mindset is a necessary illusion? The modern world plays tricks on many of our intuitions, often in ways that harm us. We crave sugar because of ecological constraints faced by our ancestors, yet sugar in the modern world is in oversupply. As empty calories become cheaper to produce than nutrient-rich foods, obesity swells into a global epidemic. Is our need to feel in control like sugar—an addictive substance that tastes good but makes us worse off overall? Or is it what drives capitalism, despite its flaws, to be such an enormously productive system for creativity and innovation? Or both? How can we begin to make sense of this part of "the human condition"?

A somewhat sad paradox: we are obsessed with efficiency and control. The looping effects of culture push us ever more forcefully into an armed defensive crouch, toward zero-sum thinking, where one person's gain is another's loss. And yet that posture may be about as effective in controlling our destinies as puffing on a pair of dice in a casino.

How can we free ourselves from this trap? Let us return to the solution Arendt offers: the ideal of action, the "miracle-working" power. If we looks up "action" in the index of *The Human Condition*, we find several entries that suggest contradictory assessments: "Action: futility of." "Action: greatness as criterion of." "Action: plurality as condition of." "Action: plurality as source of calamities of." So, we might wonder, which is it? What does Arendt really think action is all about? The answer is all of these things. Humans have an infinite capacity to start new projects. Arendt uses the metaphor of childbirth. Childbirth is "the miracle that saves the world."[39] Just as one can guide one's children but cannot control their destinies, so we launch our actions and trust them to find their own outcomes.

But herein lies action's darker side, the dangerous as well as miraculous element. We initiate actions but we almost never know how they will turn out or the reach of their consequences—hence action's "futility." The nature of action, Arendt tells us, is to upend narrowness and certainty. Action is contingent, democratic, collaborative, and unpredictable. Action shows us the spectacle of the "strong man" wrecking his little skiff on some uncharted island—all the more so when he tries to work his will on other people. Human relationships are a web, a network. *Homo faber* misunderstands this and tries to tailor the world to his designs. But the web is mighty and defeats him:

> It is because of this already existing web of human relation-ships, with its innumerable, conflicting wills and inten-tions, that action almost never achieves its purpose; but it is also because of this medium, in which action alone is real, that it "produces" stories with or without intention as natu-rally as fabrication produces tangible things. These stories may then be recorded in documents and monuments, they may be visible in use objects or art works, they may be told and retold and worked into all kinds of material.[40]

Arendt wants to resist thinking of human lives as objects that can be fashioned. We can start our stories, but we cannot dic-tate where they will end up. We need other people to interpret them with us—"to be isolated is to be deprived of the capacity to act," she writes. Though she rejects the idea of Providence as being too much like Plato's puppet-master God, she seems to think that action offers secular modern people an experience they can no longer access through religious belief: the experi-ence of a galaxy of unseen causes, unanticipated effects, and unpredictable outcomes. Arendt sees in action a secular parallel to the kind of religious conviction offered by fifteenth-century German devotional writer Thomas à Kempis: "For man pro-poses, but God disposes. The course of a man's life is not left to the man himself."

· 3 ·

Science and Humanities

Stanford students divide themselves into two camps: the "techies," students who major in engineering and the sciences, and the "fuzzies," those who major in the humanities. Though debated by students and deplored by faculty and administrators, the split has been hard-wired into the university's campus language and identity. Of course, polarization of the humanities and the sciences is by no means unique to Stanford.[1] We hear it when politicians challenge public universities to justify spending on departments outside the directly practical "STEM" fields of Science, Technology, Engineering, and Math, and when humanities scholars counter by insisting that the value of their fields transcends practical application. Defenders of the humanities insist, in the words of unexpected ally Albert Einstein, that "not everything that counts can be counted," while their detractors taunt them for offering "worthless" degrees.[2] The terms of the debate have become so familiar that speakers on both sides, however vehement or heartfelt their arguments, appear to be reading from the same script. So ingrained is this conflict on American campuses and in the American imagination that it is easy to believe it has always been with us.

Although we are literary scholars in a region that habitually celebrates the practical values of science and engineering over those of reading and reflection, our purpose in this chapter is not to defend the humanities against the sciences but to examine the conflict itself within the terms of our book's broader focus. For there is perhaps no place in contemporary culture where the age-old debate over the active life and the contemplative life is more visible and durable than in the conflict of the sciences versus the humanities. The sciences have absorbed the virtues traditionally associated with the *vita activa*: practical application toward the public good; an emphasis on productivity, utility, and outcome; and an approach to learning that has come to be called "instrumental" by both its supporters and detractors. The humanities, on the other hand, are routinely identified with the traditional values of the *vita contemplativa*: an emphasis on imagination, speculation, and reflection, and an alignment with higher values beyond the "merely" practical, political, and economic. Those who enter the conflict on either side appear to believe that it is winnable by a well-argued essay or a clever riposte. But seeing the conflict as a carry-over of the long debate over the active life versus the contemplative life helps explain why it has been and will remain so intransigent: because each side is defined against the other, each needs the other to play counterpoint. The opposition of the humanities and the sciences allows their practitioners and defenders to define themselves and the values they hold in diametrical terms: practical versus impractical, material versus idealistic, rational versus emotional, and so forth. As long as the oppositional framework remains unquestioned, any "defense" of the humanities will only end up reinforcing and prolonging the debate.

This would not pose a problem if the debate were merely a highbrow parlor game—as it has been at various stages of its long history—but the stakes now are too high to dismiss. Today, the opposition between the sciences and the humanities both stands in for and distracts from far more important questions at the center of the university's mission, which have become increasingly urgent as changing demographics, funding patterns, and modes of delivery force us to question the purpose of higher education: preparing for a job, or cultivating a life of the mind? Acquiring practical skills, or encountering great ideas? The conflict between what C. P. Snow famously called "the two cultures" will remain with us as long as we remain collectively divided about what it means to be an educated person— and judging by the ferocity of the conflict today, we are deeply divided indeed. Until we can get out from under the debate's deeply ingrained and oppositional terms, we will remain at a standstill and, most troubling of all, we will fail to respond to the urgent challenge of how to adapt the educational institutions of the past to meet the educational needs of the future.

．　．　．

Of all the criticisms leveled against the humanities, perhaps none has been more intractable than the charge of uselessness: because they lack the direct practical applications of degrees in engineering or business, insist their critics, the humanities must be a self-indulgent waste of time. Rather than refuting the charge, some practitioners of the humanities have energetically embraced it. Writing in the *New York Times'* "Opinionator" blog, Stanley Fish asserts that the uselessness of the humanities is in fact a measure of their value:

> To the question "of what use are the humanities?" the only honest answer is none whatsoever. And it is an answer

that brings honor to its subject. Justification, after all, confers value on an activity from a position outside its performance. An activity that cannot be justified is an activity that refuses to regard itself as instrumental to some larger good. The humanities are their own good.[3]

In asserting that the humanities' value is intrinsic, rather than extrinsic—conferred by "their own good," rather than serving another goal to which they are secondary—Fish calls on an argument with an ancient pedigree. In fact, the defense of "useless" knowledge goes back to the fourth century BCE, when philosophers sought to classify human intellectual activity. For Aristotle, the highest pursuit of the intellect was *theoria*, contemplation, which was "useless" or "unprofitable" because it was an end in itself—it served no higher aim, because no aim could be higher.[4] This is what Aristotle means when he insists, "To seek from all knowledge a result other than itself and to demand that knowledge must be useful is the act of one completely ignorant of the distance that from the start separates things good (which 'are loved for themselves, even if nothing else follows from them') from things *necessary* ('that are loved for the sake of something else')."[5] Contemplation is the supreme example of an undertaking that is good in itself, independent of any outcome; its "uselessness" guarantees its freedom from corruption by worldly interest. Contrasted with "useless" *theoria* is "useful" action, *praxis* or *poesis*, doing or making, which always serves another purpose. Thus, *theoria* is superior to *praxis* or *poesis*, just as the free man is superior to the slave. Aristotle's language of freedom and servitude suggests the aristocratic bias at the root of classical "liberal" education, which takes its name from the studies befitting free men, as opposed to women or slaves. It also makes the distinction between uselessness and utility foundational to the definition of "theory" and "practice," "contemplation" and "action."

This distinction between theoretical knowledge and practical or applied knowledge runs through the history of education, up to and including our current opposition of the "useful" sciences to the "useless" humanities. But as we see when we trace the debate back to Aristotle, these terms have not always held the same weighted values that they do in our age. For Aristotle, the "useless" knowledge of *theoria* was undoubtedly superior to the "useful" knowledge of *praxis*. Modernity reversed this judgment and came to value the useful over the useless, *praxis* over *theoria*. Thus Marx blames philosophers who conceive reality in "the form of an object of contemplation," rather than as "human sensuous activity [and] practice."[6]

This modern tendency to favor action over contemplation is most visible today in the relative values accorded the sciences and the humanities: whichever side they support, few would disagree that the sciences currently enjoy greater public interest, prestige, and support, precisely because of what is perceived to be their greater utility. But tracing the origins of these terms to Aristotle also recalls the fact that *theoria* and *praxis* are not exclusive to the humanities and the sciences, disciplinary categories that didn't exist in Aristotle's age—the "useless" knowledge Aristotle refers to includes geometry as well as philosophy and music. So how did the value of "useful" knowledge come to eclipse that of the "useless," and how did the two categories come to be identified with the sciences and the humanities?

Studying the past can carry the great benefit of challenging received wisdom—values we take as given—and in so doing, opening new perspectives that bring the possibility of change. We believe it is time to move past the "active sciences" versus "contemplative humanities" opposition. These terms do not reflect the range of scholarship, teaching, and learning in higher education today, nor will they advance the enterprise of higher education toward a promising future. The first step toward change is to ask how we got here, and to consider how and when things might have turned out differently.

It's easy to assume that the sciences naturally belong to the active life, or the humanities to the contemplative, but our starting point is that such values are not intrinsic to these or any other disciplines. The division between *theoria* and *praxis*—and the meanings assigned to each—both preceded the emergence of the modern disciplines and offered an elementary division through which the disciplines could be defined and legitimized. Indeed, the scientific and humanistic disciplines took shape in the modern university in reference to the ancient debate over the active life versus the contemplative life, which practitioners of each used to advance their professional claims and which led to the institutional divisions that continue to define "the humanities" against "the sciences" today. What these divisions did not do, however, was consider or serve the education of students. To the contrary, they encouraged students to perceive their education in the bifurcated terms epitomized by the division between "techies" and "fuzzies" at our own university. By considering how the humanities/sciences split draws on the active life/contemplative life split for its basic structure, terms, and values, not only can we reveal the split's submerged origins and meanings; we can also imagine new ways to organize the disciplines and the forms of learning and knowledge that they represent. In the process, we return to a question at the heart of the university's educational mission—which is not how to define and rank the relative prestige of the disciplines and their practitioners, but how best to bring the branches of learning together in order to inspire students to produce a more integrated understanding of themselves and their world.

. . .

As we have seen, the modern elevation of the "active life" over the "contemplative life" has tended to benefit the sciences over the humanities. Indeed, some scholars insist that modernity's identification with the *vita activa* was a consequence of the scientific revolution itself, which shifted popular values toward practical and worldly concerns and away from contemplative ones.[7] But in fact, a shift in the relative values of the *vita activa* and the *vita contemplativa* began long before the advent of modern science. In fourteenth-century Italy, a new curriculum emerged in the schools and universities, which carried the explicit aim of preparing its students to contribute to the practical improvement of their society. The representative philosopher for this new culture of teaching and learning was not the Greek Aristotle but the Roman Cicero, who insisted that "service is better than mere theoretical knowledge" and, by extension, that the active life of service held greater value than the contemplative life of theoretical knowledge and solitary study. As Cicero put it, "To be drawn by study away from active life is contrary to moral duty. For the whole glory of virtue is in activity."[8] The new curriculum responded to a demographic shift in the universities, as greater numbers of students entered with the intention of finding careers not in the church but in the secular business of the political and legal courts. The growing emphasis on practical education for the public good reflected this shift. Among the adherents of the new educational philosophy was Spanish humanist Juan Luis Vives, who insisted that the educated bore the responsibility to apply their education "to the use and advantage of other people," declaring, "This, then, is the fruit of all studies; this is the goal. Having acquired our knowledge, we must turn it to usefulness, and employ it for the common good."[9] This useful study, best suited to the active

life, asserted Vives and his contemporaries, wasn't science—
which was not yet recognized as its own field of study—but letters, which taught not only the high-level communication skills
essential to the lawyer and politician but also the ability to draw
from the past to make ethical decisions in the present, the basis
of what we now call "character."[10] The *studia humanitatis*, as
the new curriculum came to be known, emphasized the study of
literature, history, languages, and rhetoric—and gave the modern "humanities" their name.

Strikingly, then, the academic studies first associated with
the *vita activa* were the humanities, whose "usefulness" and application for "the common good" made them indispensable to
the professional training of a new class of secular bureaucrats.
Long before "science" emerged as a distinct discipline, the *studia humanitatis* began to assert the value of study to the active
life; in the process, humanists defined a new model of useful
learning that the sciences would later claim for themselves.
When early modern science emerged as a distinct branch of
knowledge, in other words, it did so less by introducing new
models of "active" scholarship at the expense of older "contemplative" ones than by appropriating an ideal of learning for and
as public service that was already a central humanist platform.

This point returns us to our opening assertion that neither
the sciences nor the humanities hold an intrinsic or exclusive
claim to *theoria* or *praxis*, action or contemplation. In its earliest incarnations, modern science was not clearly identifiable
with a single cultural value and place.[11] When its practitioners
sought to assign it one, they called on the preexisting categories
of "active life" and "contemplative life" that had come to define
the values of intellectual endeavor, but they displayed considerable uncertainty about which of the two was most proximate
and appropriate to the new office of the scientist: the practical
virtues of "civic" humanists, merchants, and artisans, or the

pure intellection and otherworldly detachment of medieval contemplatives.

In seventeenth-century England, the nursery of the new science was the Royal Society (originally called the College for the Promoting of Physico-Mathematical Experimental Learning), a gathering of amateur scientists who met regularly to share their experiments and discoveries. Writing in 1659, one of the society's founding members, the brilliant polymath John Evelyn, planned its headquarters on the model of a medieval monastery or contemplative community, reflecting his understanding of the work it was to carry out. He envisioned "six apartments or cells, for the members of the society . . . somewhat after the manner of the carthusians" (one of the strictest and most visionary orders of medieval monks).[12] In a similar spirit, the pioneer chemist Robert Boyle (for whom Boyle's Law is named) compared himself to a "Hermit" in his single-minded pursuit of scientific research and "averseness to society."[13] In both representations, the world of the scientist appears to be the polar opposite of that of the civic-minded humanist, inhabiting a space of detached thought as opposed to worldly engagement. Far from toppling the dominance of the *vita contemplativa*, these examples reveal that the first scientists borrowed its terms, in part to distinguish themselves from followers of the *studia humanitatis*, with their avowed commitment to the *vita activa*. This may have been strategic: the Italian humanists were famously republicans, and the English Civil War, which brought down the king, allowed humanist scholars like John Milton the opportunity to exercise their rhetorical skills in the public arena during England's short-lived and politically tumultuous Interregnum, from 1649 to 1660. Scientists, on the other hand, could assert their political neutrality by claiming a more contemplative stance, set apart from the tumult of politics.

The restoration of the monarchy with the coronation of

Charles II in 1660 marked a turning point in the rhetoric surrounding the new science, whose practitioners began to reverse their identifications with the *vita contemplativa* and to assert instead the active uses of science for the public good. John Evelyn exemplifies this shift. In *Publick Employment and an Active Life Prefer'd to Solitude* (1667), Evelyn recuperates arguments in favor of the *vita activa* from Cicero's *De officiis*, made familiar by generations of humanists, in order to stress the civic benefits of the new science.[14] Reversing his comparison, eight years earlier, of the scientific community with the monastic cloister, he insists that "the most useful and profitable of studies" partake of the active, rather than the contemplative, life: "the *Wisest men* are not made in *chambers* and *Closets* crowded with *shelves*; but by *habitudes* and active *Conversations*," he writes, suggesting that humanists, not scientists, follow a cloistered withdrawal in their studies. Against these bookish humanists, Evelyn insists that "Action is the proper fruit of *Science*," enjoining his readers:

> Let us therefore rather *celebrate* Publick *Employment* and an Active Life, which renders us so nearly ally'd to *Virtue*, *defines* and maintains our *Being, supports Societys, preserves Kingdoms* in peace, *protects* them in War; has *discover'd new Worlds, planted* the Gospel, encreases Knowledge, cultivates Arts, relieves the *afflicted*; and in sum, without which, the whole *Universe* it self had been still but a *rude* and *indigested Cäos*.[15]

As an unlikely example of such engagement, Evelyn cites Boyle, the self-proclaimed scientific hermit. Contradicting Boyle's express preference for solitary study, Evelyn insists, "If it be objected, that his employments are not *publick*, I can assure him, there is nothing more *publick*, than the *good* he's always *doing*."[16]

In elevating public-spirited scientists over the cloistered literati, Evelyn anticipates a modern habit of projecting the superiority of active over contemplative lives onto the sciences in opposition to the humanities. But his praise of civic-minded scientists, in contrast with the "letter-struck men" in their "Chambers and Closets crowded with shelves," buries its own debt to the neo-Ciceronian humanists, for whom the public virtues of the *vita activa* were grounded in the very literary study Evelyn repudiates. It also buries the contemplative models that Evelyn himself had used not long before to authorize science as a place of retreat, as distinguished from the politically engaged, humanistically oriented *vita activa*. Evelyn's example shows us that the apparent triumph of the active life over the contemplative life was not the consequence of the rise of science but its *condition*. Further, that triumph was rhetorically crafted and made commonplace by the very humanist tradition that the new science claimed to reject.

The new science may have begun to identify with the *vita activa* in order to defend against public opinion that found scientific experimentation to be fanciful and useless. Even King Charles II joked that the experimental scientists of the Royal Society were "spending time only in weighing of ayre."[17] As a contemporary named John Greenwood observed, "I have often heard it objected Against the Royall Society that though they are Ingenious men And have found out A great Many Secrets in Nature, yet what they have Done hath been Litle Advantage to the publick."[18] A less generous contemporary called science the "whimsyes of contemplative persons."[19] Faced with such criticism, and needing to secure patronage to continue their work, supporters of the Royal Society changed tactics, disavowing science's initial association with "contemplative persons" and insisting that it was instead a highly practical pursuit, despite early technological failures and scientists' own preferences for theoretical over practical work.[20] Thus Thomas Sprat's *History of the Royal Society* (1667), which historian Michael Hunter calls "a summation of polemical attempts to define the role of science in the atmosphere of the mid seventeenth century," insisted that the new science was "a Philosophy, for the use of Cities, and not for the retirements of Schools."[21]

At the same time, as the claims of science grew more practical, those of the humanities became more speculative—and oppositional. Thus the visionary eighteenth-century poet William Blake famously proclaimed, "Art is the Tree of Life. Science is the Tree of Death," pitting the imaginative against the empirical realm.[22] And in *Jerusalem*, Blake draws a contrast between the spirit of poetry and the "spectre" of science, which he embodies in modernity's foremost scientists, Sir Francis Bacon and Sir Isaac Newton:

> For Bacon and Newton, sheath'd in dismal steel, their
>   terrors hang
> Like iron scourges over Albion: reasonings like vast
>   serpents
> Infold around my limbs, bruising my minute articulations.

As the humanities and sciences emerged as separate branches of knowledge in the modern university, this mutual exclusion gave them their character and even their purpose. The modern academic cluster of fields known as "the humanities" was organized and named in direct reference to the early modern *studia humanitatis*, but despite the unbroken lineage the name implies, it became an institutional entity only in the first half of the twentieth century, when those fields were consolidated as a single division to counterbalance the growing institutional presence of the natural and social sciences. Ignoring critics who charged that the new "humanities" lacked intellectual coherence and rationale, their advocates claimed a focus on human self-understanding. In *General Education in a Free Society* (1945), the "Harvard Committee" described the humanities' mission thus: "The purpose of the humanities is to enable man to understand man in relation to himself, that is to say, in his inner aspirations and ideals."[23] This human-centered rationale contains an implicit but pointed self-defense. If, as Ralph Barton Perry explains in his "Definition of the Humanities" (1940), "humanism testifies to the eminence of man over the rest of creation," so much the more preeminent are the humanities, which are dedicated to the study of "man," over the sciences, which are dedicated to the inferior works of nature.[24] This definition, with its implicit contrast with the sciences, is still repeated in definitions of the humanities—as when Geoffrey Galt Harpham writes, "Other disciplines offer knowledge about things; the humanities offer knowledge about human beings."[25]

Such definitions set the humanities as the privileged space of the human in implicit or explicit opposition to the dehumanized sphere of the sciences, with its focus on technology, matter, and nature. Never mind that this dichotomy is challenged by the fields of neuroscience and genetics, which have made powerful contributions to our understanding of "the human," or that it ignores entire fields of the social sciences dedicated to the human, such as anthropology, psychology, and sociology. Its main function is to define the humanities in terms of what they are not (the sciences) and to claim a positive value in and through distinction from other fields of knowledge.

In the distance between the Renaissance *studia humanitatis* and the modern humanities, however, something valuable is lost: a commitment to a shared intellectual vision that cuts across disciplinary camps and upholds the goal of learning as a multifaceted, broad, and lifelong endeavor. Where the humanities' defenders today, like Harpham, stress their distinctiveness from the other fields of knowledge, Renaissance humanists stressed their necessary connection. As humanist educator Aeneas Silvius Piccolomini observed in 1450, "The disciplines are interconnected, and a person cannot master one unless he seeks light from another."[26] Others nourished understandings of the *studia humanitatis* that were sufficiently expansive as to include mathematics and biology within the domain of philosophy. In his 1570 lectures on astronomy, for example, Henry Savile insisted that "these sciences of ours should be considered, and in fact *are*, humanities (*humanitatis*)" because they advance the human quest for knowledge.[27] Without the sense of marginality that animates defenses of the humanities today, early modern humanists were free to imagine their disciplines as part of a common intellectual enterprise, not as an area distinct in its practices, objects, and increasingly well-guarded turf.

Also lost in modern definitions of the humanities is the productive balance that early modern humanists sought between knowledge and skill, *epistêmê* and *technê*. While extolling the study of philosophy as "beautiful and intellectually rewarding," early modern humanists were also obsessed with the technical points of rhetoric and grammar—and, indeed, they often portray technical skill and philosophical knowledge as two sides of the same coin. The celebrated humanist educator, Battista Guarino, refused to separate philosophical *epistêmê* from rhetorical *technê*, insisting, in words he borrows from Horace, that "knowledge is the source and principle of writing well." Likewise Pier Paolo Vergerio draws a continuum between abstract knowledge and its practical application: "The pursuit of knowledge gives birth to wondrous pleasures in the human mind and in due course bears the richest fruits."[28]

This synergy of knowledge and skill extends to the humanist ideal of a life that balances practical and theoretical knowledge to produce both wisdom and virtue, knowledge and application of the good. Humanists may have elevated the *vita activa*, but they retained the ideal of the *vita contemplativa* as an essential component of the good life. For Vergerio, such a conjunction is the ideal outcome of "liberal studies," which promote the "two kinds of life befitting a free man, one consisting entirely in leisure and contemplation, the other in action and business."[29] Indeed, students of the *studia humanitatis* were often urged to see themselves as both citizens and philosophers, with each side strengthening the other. Thus Aeneas Silvius Piccolomini could assert, "For those men alone are perfect who strive to mingle political roles with philosophy and who procure for themselves a double good: their lives are devoted to the general benefit, and, exposed to no disturbances, are spent with the greatest tranquility in the pursuit of philosophy."[30] For these *humanistae*, liberal learning—particularly its core activities of rhetoric, reading, and reflection on classical texts—did not withdraw from the world but contributed to it by producing educated individuals whose virtuous activities brought learning to life.

As Craig Kallendorf observes:

Humanist educators aimed to create a particular type of person: men and women who would be virtuous because they had read and identified with powerful examples of classical virtue; who would be prudent because they had extended their human experience into the distant past through the study of history; and who would be eloquent, able to communicate virtue and prudence to others, because they had studied the most eloquent writers and speakers of the past.[31]

In this model of humanist education, speculative knowledge and technical skill are brought together to form a third category: "Prudence," or "practical wisdom."[32] It derives from *phronêsis*, which Aristotle identifies as the action of doing informed by knowledge of human good, which bridges *epistêmê*, the action of thinking, and *technê*, the action of doing and making.[33] "Practical wisdom," as Juan Luis Vives insists, enables us to apply study "to the use and advantage of other people."[34]

In contrast with the founding figures of the *studia humanitatis*, defenders of the humanities today, like Stanley Fish, are more likely to accept the "uselessness" of their subjects, set against the practical or "instrumental" orientations identified with the sciences. In the process, they disavow the practical and technical skills that formed the bedrock of the earlier *studia humanitatis*.[35] When defenders claim that the humanities advance "the study of, contemplation of, and exploration of what it means to be a human being," they elevate contemplative knowledge while leaving out the other half of the equation, the production of technical skills.[36] Indeed, some recent defenses of the humanities explicitly separate "humanistic" from "technical" (or "instrumental") education, as if *technê* were better left to the sciences.[37]

But the deep history of the *studia humanitatis* encourages us to view the humanities as a long-term dialectic between *epistêmê* and *technê*, whose two poles, equally valuable, are necessary, though difficult, to balance. Formulating the problem this way calls the humanities to respond to the different and more interesting challenge of not just defending embattled turf but engaging in the necessary task of self-definition for a new age, which opens questions such as these: What kinds of knowledge (*epistêmê*) do the humanities produce, and what kinds of skill (*technê*)? What is the relation between the teaching of knowledge and skills and moral education (*paideia*, or *phronêsis*)? And what impact will digital cultures of literacy—not to mention visual, musical, and informational consumption—have on the epistemic and technical practices of our disciplines, as well as on our understanding of the moral and ethical challenges of the world into which we are launching our students?

In short, when the modern humanities embrace their definition as "useless," "contemplative," impractical, and nontechnical, they not only perpetuate the stalemate that now divides academic disciplines and divisions, they do so by ceding *technê*, practicality, and civic-mindedness to the sciences—disavowing qualities that played a major role in the humanities' own historical foundation. We would do better to recall the pioneers of the early modern humanities, who sought to mediate active and contemplative values, in the conviction that both practical virtue and speculative wisdom were needed by the broadly educated students they sought to produce.

At the same time, scientists might recall the associations their own predecessors made between scientific pursuit and contemplation before prioritizing practice so emphatically over theory. A disciplinary "bias against theoretical physics," for example, delayed Albert Einstein's receipt of the Nobel Prize, for which he was nominated many times before winning in 1922 (but only once his hypothesis on the photoelectric effect had been confirmed by experiments).[38] Today, many academic disciplines must defend their research against a similar privileging of empirical over theoretical methods—which Kevin A. Clarke and David M. Primo call "physics envy."[39] But a tendency to downgrade "theory" in the sciences and social sciences overlooks the importance of theoretical knowledge in its own right, as well as for its potential to contribute to practical advances. It also illustrates how, as a primary division of knowledge, the active/contemplative opposition not only separates disciplines from one another but creates further division within the disciplines themselves. Once initiated, the division of *praxis* and *theoria* is self-replicating, carving disciplines into ever-narrower slivers.

. . .

If the opposition between "practice" and "theory" has served to divide and subdivide the modern academic disciplines, those divisions do not represent the shape of knowledge in the university today. Emerging academic fields reflect a growing tendency to bring the insights of two or more disciplines together to form new lines of inquiry: bioethics combines biology and philosophy, sociobiology combines sociology and biology, and philosophy of mind combines philosophy, neuroscience, and, increasingly, computer science.[40] Similarly, the new field of optogenetics brings together the work of molecular biologists and neuroscientists to chart the work of the brain.[41] And among students from a broad range of campuses, one of the most popular new fields of study is sustainability, which can bring together diverse disciplines including history, geography, economics, city and regional planning, sociology, anthropology, and engineering.[42]

Where twentieth-century disciplines defined themselves through distinction, new fields in the twenty-first century are being produced through convergence, pursuing lines of inquiry that draw from multiple disciplines rather than confining themselves to one.[43] Such fields, and the forms of knowledge they represent, testify to the emergence of what Howard Rheingold and others call "transdisciplinary thinking." As Rheingold explains it, "transdisciplinarity goes beyond bringing together researchers from different disciplines to work in multidisciplinary teams. It means educating researchers who can speak languages of multiple disciplines."[44] More than an amalgamation of discrete disciplines (as is suggested by "multidisciplinary" or "interdisciplinary" formations), transdisciplinarity represents a way of thinking that can select perspectives, approaches, and insights from across an array of disciplines and deploy them strategically. Transdisciplinarity is less a method than a skill, one that will be increasingly "vital for workplace success," reports the Institute for the Future, an influential think tank based in Palo Alto, California. As institute researchers explain in their report *Future Work Skills 2020*, "While throughout the 20th century, ever-greater specialization was encouraged, the new century will see transdisciplinary approaches take center stage."[45] Exemplifying such an approach is UC San Diego's California Institute for Telecommunications and Information Technology (Calit2), whose collaborative projects include the Movement Laboratory, "an Art and Science Laboratory for the Study of Social Dynamics and Social Design," and the Center for Information Technology Research in the Interest of Society (CITRIS), which "creates information technology solutions for many of our most pressing social, environmental and healthcare problems."[46] Projects such as these bring together scientists, engineers, artists, humanists, and social scientists in ways that bridge traditional disciplinary divides and produce fresh approaches to complex questions.

New knowledge requires new forms of education. Where twentieth-century paradigms of teaching and learning emphasized disciplinary specialization and narrow focus, a number of influential thinkers today are calling for "a new culture of learning"—to quote the title of a recent book by Douglas Thomas and John Seely Brown—that can produce active, creative learners who are better adapted to "a world of constant change."[47] Don Tapscott draws a similar conclusion in his two in-depth studies of "the digital generation," *Growing up Digital* and *Grown Up Digital*, stressing the need for today's students to "learn how to learn, how to make sense of things that change."[48] Surveying promising new educational models in action, Thomas and Brown note that in them, students "learned much more than facts, figures, and data. They shared their interests, developed their passions, and engaged in a play of imagination." Ultimately, "what makes the concept of the new culture of learning so potent," they conclude, "is how the imagination was cultivated to harness the power of almost unlimited informational resources and create something personally meaningful."[49] The challenge we face as educators in a new era is how to restore imagination and creativity to students who have come to associate education with the lack of them—and to convince doubters that they are not just frivolous distractions but powerful and necessary human capacities.

"Imagination"—proclaims the title of a 2012 article in *Forbes*—is "What You Need to Thrive in the Future Economy."[50] Yet in the article, Rita J. King, head of business development at the consulting agency Science House, suggests that the drive to reclaim imagination may have even higher stakes: "The central question of the Imagination Age is: What does it mean to be human? This question is not easy to answer, but if we're going to guide our own evolution and preserve some aspect of our humanity in the machines we will create, we have to try." What will it take to restore imagination to a culture that has habitually belittled and marginalized it? More than installing ping-pong tables in tech offices, it requires a fundamental reconsideration of our dominant models of learning, thinking, and living. As the *Forbes* article implies (perhaps inadvertently), it also means restoring the humanities—the domain of knowledge traditionally associated with the question "What does it mean to be human?"—to areas of study, such as science and business, previously assumed to exclude them.

Schools discourage creative thinking, educator Ken Robinson observes, in large part through their tendency to "elevat[e] some disciplines over others." To counter this, "we need to eliminate the existing hierarchy of subjects. . . . The arts, sciences, humanities, physical education, languages and maths all have equal and central contributions to make to a student's education."[51] Rather than reinforce boundaries between disciplines and the value-laden hierarchies that keep them in place, we need to accept that studies in "imagination" and "humanity" are no less vital than those of "facts" and "machines." This is the time for humanists and scientists, fuzzies and techies, to overcome the divisions of knowledge, culture, and value that separate them, and to recognize that both the "practical" disciplines and the "useless" ones can benefit from cross-pollination with one another. Doing so will transform the disciplines themselves, displacing the oppositional framework that has for so long defined and divided them.

· · ·

These calls for transdisciplinary imagination—along with a new educational system that can support it—suggest a historical shift in the balance between *theoria* and *praxis*, "contemplation" and "action," that has long cemented the divisions between, and within, disciplines. It is tempting to believe that such a shift is unprecedented, that it divides us from all that has come before us. The claim of total rupture from the past is one of modernity's favorite beliefs about itself, and today's futurists and forecasters do their part to advance it. Yet our current drive toward transdisciplinary thinking in fact returns us to debates that accompanied the foundation of the modern disciplines. By revisiting these debates, we stand to discover that the modern disciplinary system we take as a given was once a far more contentious, and less univocal, institution. Recalling that the disciplines were not inevitable—that they were in fact born out of contention and have continued to shift and evolve—makes it easier to imagine our transdisciplinary future and, with it, the possibility of a more synthetic relation between sciences and humanities, active disciplines and contemplative ones.

The most influential modern spokesperson for a synthesis of the sciences and humanities was John Dewey, whose effort to harmonize theoretical and applied knowledge came at about the same time that the modern disciplines were settling into their current, divided forms. In *Democracy and Education* (1916), he criticizes what he perceives to be a growing division between the humanities and the sciences, which, he insists, "institutes an artificial separation in pupils' experience." Dewey proposes that educators "aim not at keeping science as a study apart from literature as a record of human interests, but at cross-fertilizing both the natural sciences and the various human disciplines such as history, literature, economics, and politics." Only such "cross-fertilization," he contends, could produce "a course of study which should be useful and liberal at the same time"— that is, productive of skill as well as knowledge, of practical use as well as human value.[52]

In Dewey's historical moment, public discussion around education was dominated by a battle between two camps, the "culturists" and the "utilitarians"—on the one hand, those who believed that higher education should promote great books and ideas in a realm set apart from the workaday world, and on the other, those who believed that the primary goal of education should be to prepare students to enter that world. Robert Maynard Hutchins, who championed the Great Books curriculum as president of the University of Chicago from 1929 to 1945, took the former position when he proclaimed that the university must apply itself to "the single-minded pursuit of the intellectual virtues."[53] Hutchins's imaginary adversary was Charles William Eliot, president of Harvard from 1869 to 1909, who had written:

> Universities are no longer merely students of the past, meditative observers of the present, or critics at a safe distance of the actual struggles and strifes of the working world. They are active participants in all the fundamental, progressive work of modern society. By spoken word, by pen and pencil, through laboratories, libraries, and collections, through courts, churches, schools, charities, and hospitals, they promote the forward movement of society, and help to open its onward way.[54]

Should the university be primarily a place of cloistered thought or of engaged action? Was its primary purpose to produce thinkers or workers? These questions became the focus of debates over curriculum, resource allocation, and student admission, whose polarizing terms contributed to what one contemporary observer called (in terms that felt novel in 1900) "the warfare which the 'sciences' have been waging with the 'humanities.'"[55]

Dewey entered this conflict when he took on the influential "social efficiency" movement of the early twentieth century.[56] The movement called for a curriculum that met the needs of the new industrial society by preparing students more directly for their future occupational roles, determined by their class background and gender. Thus it separated liberal education, imagined as the space of leisured thinking, from vocational education, the space of active doing, and assigned them respectively to the elite and working classes. The movement's spokesman was David Snedden, a Stanford-educated reformer, who distinguished between vocational and liberal education on the basis of class: "Vocational education may be designed to make a person an efficient producer; liberal education may be designed to make him an effective consumer or user."[57] Both vocational and liberal education were directed toward the effective performance of social roles: vocational, by offering to the "rank and file" "that utilitarian training which looks to individual efficiency in the world of work"; liberal, by instilling principles of taste that would allow society's leaders to become effective consumers.[58] No academic study, Snedden insisted, could be "regarded as an end in itself"—instead, he advocated an "education more nearly related to the necessities of the active life."[59]

The bifurcated curriculum favored by Snedden and his colleagues took vocational preparation to an extreme: while encouraging study in "agricultural, business, clerical, industrial, fine-arts, and household-arts curriculums," Snedden called for vocational education to be divided into ever narrower subfields:

> tailoring, jewelry salesmanship, poultry farming, coal cutting, stationary engine firing, waiting on table (hotel), cutting (in shoe factory), automobile repair, teaching of French in secondary school, mule spinning, power machine operating (for ready made clothing), raisin grape growing, general farming suited to Minnesota, linotype composition, railway telegraphy, autogenous welding, street car motor driving, and a hundred others.[60]

The many jobs in Snedden's model curriculum that were destined for obsolescence indicate a major shortcoming of vocational education: in its desire to meet specific social needs, it fails to prepare students for changing circumstances. Nonetheless, the views of the social efficiency movement came to dominate American education. As educational historian Diane Ravitch observes, "Snedden's advocacy of curricular differentiation based on pupils' occupational destination (and gender) rapidly entered the mainstream of educational thought, as did his disparagement of learning for its own sake; his views concurred with those of industrialists and those who thought of themselves as practical."[61] President Theodore Roosevelt reflected the influence of the social efficiency movement when in 1907 he wrote to Henry S. Pritchett, president of the new National Society for the Promotion of Industrial Education, to express his support of the society's aims: "We of the United States must develop a system under which each individual citizen shall be trained so as to be effective individually as an economic unit and fit to be organized with his fellows so that he and they can work in efficient fashion together."[62]

The influence of Snedden and the social efficiency movement remains visible today. "What we ended up with," historian David F. Labaree observes, "was a school system that reflected the main elements of the social efficiency agenda: a differentiated curriculum, de facto tracking by social class, and a school system whose purpose is viewed through a vocational lens (education for human capital development)."[63] By the end of the twentieth century, according to Herbert M. Kliebard, the program of the social efficiency movement constituted a rationale for all of higher education, transforming "the curriculum as a whole in line with the criteria and protocols of the workplace."[64]

While Snedden disparaged educational progressives like Dewey, whose reforms (he claimed) were based on "mystic principles of 'character,' 'self-realization,' or 'disciplined mind,'" it would be wrong to charge Dewey with lacking interest in students' occupational direction.[65] To the contrary, Dewey observed that "perhaps the most important problem in education is to [balance] ... occupational direction with a genuinely liberal content," to equip students not only with practical capabilities of doing, but also with intellectual capabilities of reflecting on and understanding the significance of what they are doing—"with a sense of the social and moral applications [that their actions] potentially possess."[66] A separation of practical and vocational education from liberal education, of "doing" from "thinking," reinstates the traditional division of action and contemplation that, Dewey insists, education in the true sense must bridge:

> The reactionary critics are busy urging that the [practical and vocational] subjects be taught to the masses—who are said to be incapable of rising to the plane of the "intellectual" but who do the useful work which somebody has to do, and who may be taught by vocational education to do it more effectively. This view is of course an open and avowed attempt to return to that dualistic separation of ideas and action, of the "intellectual" and the "practical," of the liberal and servile arts, that marked the feudal age.[67]

Instead of meeting the argument for vocational education with a counterargument for liberal education, Dewey insists that the division itself is both false and destructive and calls on his readers to rethink the terms on which the conflict is founded.

Dewey's background and training was in philosophy, and he understood contemporary debates on education in the context of long-running philosophical disputes over the *vita activa* and the *vita contemplativa*. In his writing, he continually blames the modern separation of action and contemplation for both the failures of modern education and their social consequences. Dewey traces the origins of the division to the work of Greek philosophers, in which "the realms of knowledge and action were each divided into two regions," but he also insists that "it is not to be inferred that Greek philosophy separated activity from knowing. It connected them."[68] In contrast, he argues, modernity has created an unbridgeable chasm between them. This "alleged separation of knowing and doing," he argues, has resulted in a deeply divided educational system.[69]

As Dewey observes, "A mental review of the intellectual presuppositions underlying the oppositions in education of labor and leisure, theory and practice, body and mind, mental states and the world, will show that they culminate in the antithesis of vocational and cultural education."[70] The split, that is, undermines both education for practical work (vocational) *and* education for abstract knowledge (cultural). Its consequences are both intellectual and social. Intellectually, Dewey objects to the separation of knowing and doing as a subversion of genuine learning: "It can be shown that the actual procedures by which the most authentic and dependable knowledge is attained have completely surrendered the separation of knowing and doing."[71] Following this observation, he offers a model of educational reform in which "action is at the heart of ideas" and "knowing itself is a form of action."[72] Reuniting action and knowledge, he asserts, will break down the artificial barriers that separate the applied disciplines from the theoretical ones and encourage students to recognize the mutual dependence of active and reflective learning.

The modern tendency to separate knowing and doing, contemplation and action, was a recent development, Dewey insisted. As a precedent for his own thinking on education and a harbinger of the educational alternatives he envisioned, he recalled the Renaissance polymath Francis Bacon—"the great forerunner of the spirit of modern life."[73] Dewey's identification with Bacon establishes him as the heir of the early modern humanists who aspired to achieve a synthesis of action and contemplation. This was an ideal that Bacon set for himself. As he admitted in a letter to Isaac Casaubon in 1609, he intended his "contemplations" to bear fruit in the world of action: "For indeed to write at leisure that which is to be read at leisure matters little; but to bring about the better ordering of man's life and business, with all its troubles and difficulties, by the help of sound and true contemplations—that is the thing I aim at."[74]

Further anticipating Dewey, Bacon expresses concern that his contemporaries are beginning to separate contemplation and action into conflicting camps. He illustrates this point in a jarring allegory:

> After the fall of man, we see ... an image of the two estates, the contemplative state and the active state, figured in the two persons of Abel and Cain, and in the two simplest and most primitive trades of life; that of the shepherd (who, by reason of his leisure, rest in a place, and living in view of heaven, is a lively image of a contemplative life), and that of the husbandman.[75]

Bacon's novel interpretation of a biblical story of fratricidal conflict recalls classical treatments of active and contemplative lives by aligning them with the pastoral and georgic poetic genres, the literary forms of leisure (the shepherd) and work (the tiller of fields). But it also presents the brothers as opposed figures of intellectual labor, contrasting Abel's detached watchfulness and Cain's active ingenuity: the one, aloof, contemplative, and favored by God, the other, active, worldly, and cursed.

In contrast to the violent opposition of action and contemplation implicit in this reading, Bacon proposes a new model of intellectual synthesis in a project that he calls a "Georgics of the mind." The term directly recalls Cain, the husbandman and "tiller of the ground" (the root meaning of "georgic"), redeeming his active labor by aligning it with the intellectual pursuits of Adam and Abel:

> And surely if the purpose be in good earnest not to write at leisure that which men may read at leisure, but really to instruct and suborn action and active life, these Georgics of the mind, concerning the husbandry and tillage thereof, are no less worthy than the heroical descriptions of Virtue, Duty, and Felicity.[76]

Bacon's "Georgics of the mind" imagines thinking as inextricably linked to doing, as an action in its own right that disciplines and guides the active life, rather than standing apart from it. In the process, Bacon recuperates the humanist ideal of *phronesis*, practical wisdom, which reconciles knowledge and action in the life of the truly educated.

. . .

Dewey attempts to adapt Bacon's model to twentieth-century education. The stakes are high: not only would such a reform involve students more actively in their education, he insists; it would also remedy the social consequences that follow from the bifurcation of knowing and doing, culture and utility. "Traditionally," Dewey observes, education in "liberal culture has been linked to the notions of leisure, purely contemplative knowledge, and a spiritual activity not involving the active use of bodily organs." This is sharply differentiated from the method and milieu of purely vocational education, by which "some people are trained by suitable practical exercises for capacity in doing things, for ability to use the mechanical tools involved in turning out physical commodities and rendering personal service."[77] The separation of thinkers from doers or makers follows from the assumption that thought belongs to a leisured class, a model we can trace to Aristotle's aristocratic elevation of *theoria* over *praxis* and *poeisis*. Against this model, Dewey asserts the necessity of a fully developed education to "a truly democratic society," which he identifies as one "in which all share in useful service and all enjoy worthy leisure." This unity of useful service and worthy labor can only be realized, he insists, through "educational transformation."[78]

Though an enthusiastic supporter of the experimental sciences, Dewey never advocates for them at the expense of the humanities, because, as he insists, "there is no kind of inquiry which has a monopoly of the honorable title of knowledge. The engineer, the artist, the historian . . . by their fruits we shall know them."[79] Instead, he critiques practitioners of science for claiming "invidious monopolies" and a "privileged relation to the real."[80] Against the claim that "science is the only valid kind of knowledge," Dewey observes that "it is just an intensified form of knowing in which are written large the essential characters of any knowing." The power of experimental inquiry to bridge doing and knowing, he insists, should be the aim of all disciplines, yet "our logic in social and humane subjects is still largely that of definition and classification as until the seventeenth century it was in natural science."[81] By comparing the modern humanities with the early modern sciences, he holds out hope that the humanities will experience a renewal in the same way that science did in the age of Bacon.

In imagining this renewal, Dewey offers a vision of truly transdisciplinary knowledge that bridges artificial distinctions of learning as well as the social divisions they produce.[82] He challenges educators to look beyond "the existing conflict between the sciences and the humanities in the contemporary college curriculum" and to recognize that "in spite of confusion and conflict, the movement of the human mind is a unity. The development of the new sciences is not a mere addition of so much bulk of information to what went before. It represents a profound modification and reconstruction of all attained knowledge—a change in quality and standpoint," the profound impact of which must be registered in the humanistic fields as well. Dewey insists that human thought and knowledge overflow the boundaries imposed on them by the academic disciplines. He holds it to be the duty of all disciplines to register and respond to changes in any field of knowledge: "The body of knowledge is indeed one; it is a spiritual organism. To attempt to chop off a member here and amputate an organ there is the veriest impossibility. The problem is not one of elimination, but of organization; of simplification not through denial and rejection, but through harmony."[83]

We hear echoes of Dewey's appeal to a syncretic body of knowledge in today's calls for curricula responsive to the growing transdisciplinarity of new fields of knowledge. And we see his appeal for a reintegration of vocational and liberal education in the recent efflorescence of "integrative" models of teaching and learning, which encourage students to integrate practical experience and reflective thought. As Carol Geary Schneider, former president of the American Association of Colleges and Universities, writes, "It is time to tear down the walls that have traditionally divided liberal education from pre-professional fields, and to make a commitment to teach every field as a form of liberal or liberating education."[84] Other educators have called for renewed emphasis on liberal learning within the undergraduate business major, which remains the most popular field of study in American colleges and universities today. Anne Colby, Thomas Ehrlich, William M. Sullivan, and Jonathan R. Dolle observe that instrumental thinking currently dominates undergraduate business education, wherein "every course is judged by its apparent value as a means toward academic and, eventually, career success."[85] Such an approach, they argue, denies students training in conceptual, reflective, and abstract thought that would allow them to understand their pragmatic goals within larger frames of meaning and to bring to those goals the benefit of a full array of analytical skills. On the other hand, they observe:

> Although a judgment about particular problems of practice must serve technical and pragmatic ends, in order for it to count as good professional judgment, it cannot be entirely instrumental. That is, professional judgment must not only be guided by rich knowledge and strong technical skills, it must also be aligned with the public purposes, ethical principles, and ideals of the profession.[86]

Such capacities, reached through reflection, integration, and critical analysis, are fostered through liberal education and fulfilled in what the authors, echoing Renaissance humanists, call "*practical wisdom* . . . embodied in wise, capable, and thoughtful practice."[87] This term, we might recall, is the same one humanists use to translate Aristotle's *phronêsis*, which we defined earlier as the mediation of speculative knowledge and technical skill, or the ability to act informed by knowledge of human good. "Practical wisdom," to recall humanist Juan Luis Vives, enables us to apply the fruits of our study "to the use and advantage of other people." As such, it represents the culmination of an education that balances theory and practice to produce the highest wisdom of which humans are capable.

What would it mean to take Dewey's vision of an education that unites thinking and doing as a new plan of action for teaching, learning, and knowledge in our increasingly transdisciplinary world? To start, it would mean dropping the oppositional models of the past and considering the sciences and the humanities, the applied and the theoretical disciplines, as interrelated facets of a larger whole. Instead of defining the humanities and theoretical sciences as "useless," in opposition to the "useful" sciences and engineering, we might instead reaffirm the many ways in which theoretical and applied knowledge coexist and strengthen one another both within and across disciplines.[88] And instead of opposing liberal education to professional education, we might reconsider how practical studies could be deepened and enriched through integration with the reflective, interpretive, and contextual ways of thinking represented by the humanities. Above all, it would mean overcoming the polarized and polarizing rhetoric that pits "action" against "contemplation," impoverishing both the humanities and the sciences. By replacing opposition with "cross-pollination," we might conceive human knowledge within a dynamic ecosystem and acknowledge the prescience of Dewey's observation that the challenge facing universities and those who care about them—whether as teachers or students, administrators or parents, politicians or citizens—is advancing the common goal and vision that binds fields of knowledge and enables coherent and mutually productive relationships between them.

In an era of competition for diminished resources, both within and across campuses, such cross-institutional thinking has become rare, though all the more necessary. Yet many universities and colleges are meeting this challenge; in the process, they have helped to reclaim the liberal arts ideal of holistic, integrated studies for our time. Their campuses are not only student-focused but take the development of students' full humanity as their central mission. In this, they might be guided by Wendell Berry, who calls for a renewal of the humanizing mission at the university's core:

> The thing being made in a university is humanity. . . . [W]hat universities . . . are mandated to make or to help to make is human beings in the fullest sense of those words— not just trained workers or knowledgeable citizens but responsible heirs and members of human culture. . . . Underlying the idea of a university—the bringing together, the combining into one, of all the disciplines—is the idea that good work and good citizenship are the inevitable by-products of the making of a good—that is, a fully developed—human being.[89]

Berry's call for a university of humanity could also recall the humanities to their Renaissance roots. For the original *studia humanitatis* focused not on "knowledge about human beings," despite the insistence of defenders of the humanities today, but on humanity—which they studied not as an object, but as a defining goal. The *humanitatis* at the term's heart doesn't refer to a preexisting "human" quality (like "human dignity" or "the human experience") but to the classical Latin meaning of *humanus* as both "benevolent" and "learned." This humanity is not "discovered" but deliberately cultivated through education. Thus the humanist educator Battista Guarino writes in 1459:

To mankind has been given the desire to know, which is also where the humanities get their name. For what the Greeks call *paideia* we call learning and instruction in the liberal arts. The ancients also called this *humanitas*, since devotion to knowledge has been given to the human being alone out of all living creatures.[90]

Rather than study of the human *qua* human, *studia humanitas* signified "the humane studies or the studies befitting a human being."[91] The goals of the early humanists—the *humanistae* who taught the *studia humanitatis*—were both idealistic and practical. They aimed to build students' character through liberal learning (the meaning of *paideia*) and to prepare them for a world of massively expanded literacy and immense complexity, where the skills of communication, interpretation, and the negotiation of practical ethical problems were of paramount importance. To these early educators, the reconciliation of the active life and the contemplative life was the goal of all truly educated people, since it would enable them to unite the fruits of their studies with the urgent needs of their own societies. In calling for a reconciliation of thinking and doing, Dewey is right to turn to Bacon for his model, even if Bacon's project would remain incomplete in the Renaissance, just as Dewey's has in our time.

· 4 ·

Work and Leisure

Every year, UCLA's Higher Education Research Institute produces a well-publicized report entitled *The American Freshman*, which surveys the attitudes of the nation's incoming college students about their personal and educational goals. And every year, one of the survey's findings receives considerable attention: among a list of "objectives considered to be essential or very important," students now rank "to be very well off financially" above "to develop a meaningful philosophy of life," reversing the relative ratings of these goals in the late 1960s, when the report was first issued.

This reversal is consistently taken to signal the crass careerism of college students today, who pursue material gain—the perception goes—at the expense of learning to think for themselves. As Emory English professor Mark Bauerlein lamented in the *New York Times* after the release of the 2014 survey, "Finding meaning and making money have traded places."[1] Ten years earlier, an opinion piece in the *Chicago Tribune* had drawn the same conclusion: "They'd love to ponder the meaning of life. Really, they would. But pondering takes so much time, doesn't pay well, and offers lousy fringe benefits. So they'd rather just get on with . . . the business of making money."[2] In the logic of accounts like this, the survey represents a zero-sum game: "making money" cancels out "pondering." One's gain is the other's loss.

Yet the actual data tell a different, and more interesting, story. While ratings of the goal "to be very well off financially" as important have indeed climbed—from 51.1 percent in 1967 to 82.3 percent in 2016—those of "to develop a meaningful philosophy of life" have also risen. After falling from a high of 84.8 percent in 1967 (the first year the question was asked) to 40.7 percent in 1986, the figure has moved up again, reaching 44.8 percent in 2016.[3] More unexpectedly still, "develop-[ing] a meaningful philosophy of life" now receives its highest ratings—more than ten points higher than the overall averages—in historically black colleges and universities (HBCUs)—where it now stands at 55.9 percent, contradicting the assumption that the search for philosophical meaning is restricted to a small and privileged elite. In other words, while commentators see philosophical and material goals as incompatible, if not diametrically opposed, students themselves do not. According to a report analyzing forty-year trends in the *American Freshman* survey, the data indicate "that students . . . are seeking ways to bring meaning into their lives at the same time they encounter strong pressures for economic success."[4] The challenge today's students define for themselves isn't choosing "economic success" at the expense of "meaning," then, but bringing both values together into a well-balanced life.

This point is supported by the remaining survey results. When asked about the purpose of higher education, the students rate "to be able to get a better job" at 84.8 percent, only one point higher than "to learn more about things that interest me," which checks in at 83.8 percent. And the desire "to make more money," at 72.6 percent, is actually valued less than "to gain a general education and appreciation of ideas," rated as "very important" by 75.4 percent of the students.[5]

Moreover, the survey shows that students place increasingly high value on other nonmaterialistic goals: "helping others in difficulty" was valued by 77.5 percent in 2016, the highest figure in thirty years (up from 48 percent in 1986).[6] Steady gains also appear for creative and imaginative goals, such as "becoming accomplished in one of the performing arts" (12 percent in 1986, 17.5 percent in 2016), "writing original works" (13 percent in 1986, 18.2 percent in 2016), and "creating artistic works" (11.8 percent in 1986, 17.7 percent in 2016). These are not the values of students in pursuit of "the unexamined but affluent life," as the *Chicago Tribune* op-ed put it, but students whose desire for professional success leaves room for meaningful intellectual, altruistic, and creative goals.

The mismatch between students' attitudes and their interpretation in the popular press reflects a generational gap in thinking about the relation between the practical arena of work and the philosophical and personal search for meaning—or, in the terms of this book, between action and contemplation. Evidently it is easier for commentators to imagine these values locked in conflict than it is to understand a generation hoping to integrate them. But such commentators have the weight of history behind them, while the young face the challenge of inventing new paradigms. A long tradition separates professional success from philosophical meaning, "making money" from "pondering." Today's students are not immune from that history—indeed, we often see our own students wrestling with its incapacitating legacy. But their efforts to imagine their way out of its trap also signal the emergence of a new attitude, one that hopes to synthesize philosophical meaning and professional success, personal fulfillment and material well-being. This attitude is quietly rewriting the old myths, though we need to look harder—as we will do in this chapter—to discover the new possibilities it brings to life.

. . .

The long-standing division between work and philosophical reflection is recorded in the very terms we use to describe them. In the classical and medieval periods, *otium* meant cultivated leisure, time free from worldly employment that could be devoted to intellectual or spiritual development; *negotium* meant its opposite, work that was identified as a lack or disturbance of such valuable leisure. Since "neg-" means "not," *negotium* literally means "not-leisure." But in later modernity the terms' meanings shifted: the positive values attached to *otium* were replaced by the negative values now carried by the term "otiose." Leisure came to be seen not as cultivated and meaningful but as an ineffectual, fruitless, and impractical waste of time. At the same time, *negotium* shed its earlier, negative definition as the absence of leisure and came to mean skilled commercial or social transactions, now identified with the world of business: negotiation. In our own age, the survival of "negotiation" as a positive term and "otiose" as a negative one records the persistence of cultural values that place work above leisure, action above contemplation. So, too, does the near-obsolescence of the once-prized *otium*, whose nearest surviving lexical relative, "leisure," is doomed to cultural irrelevance through unfortunate associations with seventies-era sports clothing or temperate retirement communities.

The twentieth century saw a partial effort to redeem *otium* and the values of cultivated leisure it once represented. Recalling, without contradicting, economist Thorstein Veblen's definition of leisure as the "non-productive consumption of time," philosopher Josef Pieper insists that leisure was "the basis of culture."[7] Pieper protests the modern degradation of "leisure" as "another word for laziness, idleness, and sloth." To the contrary, he insists, "Leisure . . . is not a Sunday afternoon idyll, but the preserve of freedom, of education and culture, and of that undiminished humanity which views the world as a whole."[8] In a similar vein, Sebastian de Grazia, a political scientist whose *Of Time, Work, and Leisure* (1962) argues eloquently for recuperating the *vita contemplativa*, insists that "the benefits of leisure are the benefits of cultivating the free mind," which can be measured in the production of "creativeness, truth, and freedom."[9]

Both accounts redeem *otium* by distinguishing it from work. Thus Pieper juxtaposes the ideal state of "leisure" with the "spiritually impoverished" state of "total work," while De Grazia insists that "the world is divided into two classes," on the one side, "the practical man" and "the businessman," on the other, the "man of leisure" who "love[s] ideas and imagination."[10] In the view of sociologist C. Wright Mills, whose *White Collar: The American Middle Classes* (1951) dissects the ethos of midcentury bureaucratic culture, the middle-class worker suffers from a "deep-rooted malaise" brought on by his alienation from the high-order benefits of leisure: "The faculties of reflection, imagination, dream, and desire, so far as they exist, do not now move in the sphere of concrete, practical work experience."[11] The mid-twentieth century may have succeeded in redeeming "leisure," but it did so only by heightening its contrast with work, making leisure a place of imagination, fulfillment, and culture, in opposition to the blind conformity and materialism of the middle-class American workplace.

If popular cultural narratives of the 1960s reinforced this split by rejecting the white-collar workplace, the 1970s broached the

possibility that work itself could foster levels of personal fulfillment previously restricted to the "nonwork" realm of leisure.
With his phenomenally popular job-hunter's manual, *What
Color Is Your Parachute?* (1970), Richard Nelson Bolles introduced a surprising premise: our work itself has the potential
to bring us deep meaning and happiness, not just the money
with which to purchase the moments of leisure where meaning and happiness reside apart. Every successful job search,
Bolles insists, begins with the question "Who am I?"—or, as an
alternative, What, if I lost it, would cause life to have no meaning?[12] With this, Bolles infuses the job search with levels of inquiry that previously belonged to philosophy. For Plato's Socrates, the philosopher's first injunction is "know thyself." But this
was a question undertaken in contemplation—the place where,
for Aristotle, true happiness, *eudaimonia*, dwells. In the Western tradition, work was something else entirely. As we read in
Ecclesiastes, "The labor of man does not satisfy the soul." By
insisting that the right job can bring meaning, happiness, and
self-knowledge, *What Color Is Your Parachute?* claims the traditional values of the *vita contemplativa* for the *vita activa*—and in
the process, collapses the binary opposition that had come to
define the terms.

The idea that true work has the potential to fulfill us, to bring
us happiness and to give our lives meaning, takes us far from
the self-alienating workplace described by Mills twenty years
earlier—and it continues to infuse popular discussions of work
today. Po Bronson's bestselling *What Should I Do with My Life?*
(2002) recounts the stories of "people who answered the ultimate question," in language that borrows from narratives of
spiritual quest or that is otherwise identified with the *vita contemplativa*: his subjects' search for meaningful work is driven by
their need to discover their "passion," "mission," "calling," and
"higher purpose." When one subject discovers his vocation, his

"face radiated enlightenment."[13] Alain de Botton's *The Pleasures and Sorrows of Work* (2009) marvels at work's "extraordinary claim to be able to provide us, alongside love, with the principal source of life's meaning."[14] And Chade-Meng Tan's *Search inside Yourself* (2012), drawing from a meditation-based course the author leads for Google employees, promises that "your work will become a source of your happiness" only if it is "work [that] is deeply meaningful to you."[15] This value permeates the new professional technology culture. According to a recent profile, media entrepreneur Tim O'Reilly "says he has tried to use his company to demonstrate that being an entrepreneur can represent a means of exploring the world, one that is just as profound as religious inquiry or Greek philosophy or New Age introspection. 'Business doesn't have to be separated from the rest of life,' he says."[16]

In a movement that began with *What Color Is Your Parachute?* and continues to the present, we are witnessing a profound shift in ideas about the relative meanings of the active life and contemplative life and what they mean for work and its place in life and society. This development is comparable in importance to the reversal in relative meanings of *otium* and *negotium* from the classical period to the Renaissance; but while that shift only reversed the priority of these two terms, the current search for meaningful work seeks to knit the two into one. Imagined as a source of deep happiness and self-knowledge, the idea of meaningful work simultaneously embodies active-life and contemplative-life values. Meaningful work produces both utility and transcendent meaning; it links the practical good and the philosophical good. But it can be hard to wrap our heads around, inducing confusion at best, and at worst, cynical manipulation. With barely a nod to the centuries-old distinction that he seems to obscure, Google's Chade-Meng Tan asks, "What if people can also use contemplative practices to help them succeed in life and at work? In other words, what if contemplative practices can be made beneficial both to people's careers and to business bottom lines?"[17] The statement is dizzying in its incoherence, since contemplation is, by definition, non-instrumental—a practice undertaken for its own sake and intrinsic value, not for the achievement of a goal. When "contemplative practices" are made into tools for achieving career success and improving the bottom line, we appear to have reached the bleak reality diagnosed by Hannah Arendt, where all value reduces to market value, and contemplation—together with any intrinsically meaningful activity—means nothing, on its own terms, at all.

But the search for deeply meaningful work remains a driving goal of our time, and as such, it represents a new chapter in the ongoing philosophical debate over the active life and the contemplative life. Economist E. F. Schumacher's classic treatment of the subject, *Good Work*, insists "that work is the joy of life and is needed for our development, but that meaningless work is an abomination." As Schumacher defines it, good work is intrinsically selfless, connecting the worker with a larger realm of deep meaning and value: "In the process of doing good work the ego of the worker disappears. He frees himself from his ego, so that the divine element in him can become active."[18] This definition of work as connection to a deep, even divine, sense of meaning and purpose—as a contemplative pursuit in itself—invites us to rethink a complex of ideas that insists on the separation of work and contemplation. For example, while contemplation has long been associated with solitude and work with sociality, imagining a category of contemplative work also means rethinking in a fundamental way what we mean by individual selfhood, collective society, and the relation between the two.

If the new culture of work urges individuals to seek personal fulfillment in their jobs, the nature of work is also challenging the ego-driven workplace. Conditioned by digital fluency and social media, the (so-called) millennial generation to which our students belong is catalyzing this change, we are told, by demanding different models of community at work. Morley Winograd and Michael D. Hais report that "millennials are determined to change the world of work once and for all" by moving away from "the overall command-and-control approach to organizing work, introduced by America's last civic generation." Young workers, the authors observe, are not driven by the "ego or sense of rank" that motivated their seniors.[19] Thomas W. Malone predicts that the millennial-driven "new order of business" will change the old by "loosening the hierarchy" and "harnessing democracy" in ways that develop out of social media and Silicon Valley start-up culture.[20] And Don Tapscott and Anthony D. Williams see the future of work in "mass collaboration."[21] Such changes to the social organization of the workplace can only further transform the meaning of work for the individuals who enter it, as well as the nature of the personal needs and desires they bring to it. What will such seismic shifts in thinking about work and the individual mean for, and within, the long-standing debate over action and contemplation, *negotium* and *otium*, that we have been tracing?

. . .

As our thinking shifts about work and leisure, action and contemplation, so do the stories we tell to make sense of those shifts. As new paradigms of work emerge, new parables are appearing on the culture's ground floor—that is, in stories directed at young people, which have long been the places where cultures articulate and instruct their most basic values.[22]

The meanings and relative values of work and leisure have been taught to children over millennia through the well-known fable "The Grasshopper and the Ants," which entered modernity in the well-known version by seventeenth-century French fabulist Jean de la Fontaine, "La Cigale et la Fourni" ("The Cicada and the Ant"):

La cigale ayant chanté
Tout l'été,
Se trouva fort dépourvue
Quand la bise fut venue:
Pas un seul petit morceau
De mouche ou de vermisseau.
Elle alla crier famine
Chez la fourmi sa voisine,
La priant de lui prêter
Quelque grain pour subsister
Jusqu'à la saison nouvelle.
« Je vous paierai, lui dit-elle,
Avant l'août, foi d'animal,
Intérêt et principal. »
La fourmi n'est pas prêteuse:
C'est là son moindre défaut.
« Que faisiez-vous au temps chaud?
Dit-elle à cette emprunteuse.
—Nuit et jour à tout venant
Je chantais, ne vous déplaise.
—Vous chantiez ? J'en suis fort aise :
Eh bien ! Dansez maintenant. »

Cicada, having sung her song
All summer long
Found herself without a crumb
When winter winds did come.
Not a scrap was there to find

Of fly or earthworm, any kind.
Hungry, she ran off to cry,
To neighbor Ant, and specify:
Asking for a loan of grist,
A seed or two so she'd subsist.
Just until the coming spring.
She said, "I'll pay you everything
Before fall, my word as animal.
Interest and principal."
Well, no hasty lender is the Ant;
It's her finest virtue by a lot.
"And what did you do when it was hot?"
She then asked this mendicant.
"To all comers, night and day,
I sang. I hope you don't mind."
"You sang? Why, my joy is unconfined.
Now dance the winter away."[23]

La Fontaine's version stresses the contrast between the hard-working ant and the begging cicada, emphasizing the lesson that we must put work before pleasure to earn our rest.

Although popularly attributed to Aesop, the fable circulated widely in many Greek and Latin versions, with the best-known bearing the name of the fifth-century AD fabulist, Avianus.[24] Across its earliest retellings, the fable's advocacy of hard work over wasteful leisure remains constant. There are, however, considerable variations in the main characters (the grasshopper is alternately a cicada, a dung beetle, or a cricket) and in the particular offense of which the wasteful insect is guilty. Take, for example, "The Ant and the Dung Beetle":

During the summer, the ant went around the fields collecting grains of wheat and barley so that he could store up some food for the winter. A dung beetle watched the ant and decided that he must be a wretched creature since he worked all the time, never taking a moment's rest, unlike the other animals. The ant didn't pay attention to the dung beetle and simply went about his business. When winter came and the dung was washed away by the rain, the beetle grew hungry. He went to the ant and begged him to share a little bit of his food. The ant replied, "O beetle, if you had done some work yourself instead of making fun of me while I was working so hard, then you would not need to be asking me for food."

The fable teaches us that we should not neglect important things that require our attention, and instead we should attend in good time to our future well-being.[25]

In this version, the dung beetle exemplifies those who value useless material possessions over the things necessary to sustenance. Thus the Cynic philosopher Crates—who famously shed all his wealth in order to devote himself to philosophy—gently satirizes those who "heap up the wealth of the beetle," whose treasures amount to dung.[26] The fable's emphasis on the virtue of hard work mirrors the philosophy of the Cynics, who glorified the life of *ponos*, toil, over rest and luxury.

The theme was not uncommon: in a similar vein, the early Greek poet Hesiod condemns idleness and praises work in his didactic poem *Works and Days*:

Hunger is altogether a meet comrade for the sluggard. Both gods and men are angry with a man who lives idle, for in nature he is like the stingless drones who waste the labour of the bees, eating without working; but let it be your care to order your work properly, that in the right season your barns may be full of victual. Through work men grow rich in flocks and substance, and working they are much better loved by the immortals. Work is no disgrace: it is idleness which is a disgrace.[27]

Like the teller of "The Ant and the Dung Beetle," Hesiod suggests that the idle should be punished with hunger. His praise of work over idleness contains an implicit critique of the aristocratic elite, who, like drones, live off the work of others, "eating without working." Hesiod's contrast between parasitic, idle men and hardworking, virtuous ones is consistent with the ethos of Athenian democracy, whose supporters frequently invoked images of working communities in nature, like the bees in Hesiod or the ants in the fable, to support the idea of a society sustained by the participation of its citizens.

This opposition of work and idleness begs the question of what counts as a productive labor. By describing the philosopher's life as one of *ponos*, Crates differentiates himself from Aristotle, who celebrated the philosopher's aloofness from the world of work—and in so doing, caused others, like the playwright Aristophanes, to satirize contemplative philosophers as "idle fellows and good for nothings."[28] The question of useful work versus useless leisure hangs over the fable, becoming increasingly prominent in its later retellings. While the figure of the hard-working ant remains relatively stable, the identity of her nonworking companion changes, from the dung-hoarding beetle to a musical insect, whose "occupation" is as ambiguous as that of the philosopher.

Other early versions of the fable retain its praise of industry over idleness, but they differ in how they apply its lessons to the well-lived life. William Caxton's "Of the Ant and the Sygale" (1484) champions its hard-working ant against the musical grasshopper but falls short of condemning singing per se, arguing instead for balance: "there is one tyme for to doo some labour and werk / And one tyme for to have rest." Another medieval translator, Marie de France, challenges readers to consider the relative values of community and individual self-interest that the fable represents. Her cricket admits that he "sang and played with other insects" all summer but, come winter, finds that his friends have abandoned him: "now I find no one who will shelter me." The ant chides the cricket for neglecting to "provide for yourself," a lesson that the moral drives home: "Each person should take care to store up his wealth, doing what must be done. It is better to have what is sufficient to your needs than to expect it from others."29

Marie's translation appeared at a time when medieval Europe was turning away from traditional forms of community care and leaving individuals to fend for themselves, igniting debates about the common versus the personal good that are reflected in her retelling of the fable. But Marie also identifies a paradox that would continue to trouble the fable's later readers and translators: in her single-minded attention to productive work, the ant appears to shirk the responsibilities of charity, advocating a vision of society that is both cruel and joyless. The fable depicts a conflict not only between work and idleness, but between toil and pleasure, self-sufficiency and community, bare survival and all the things that make life worth living.

La Fontaine himself registers unease with the ant's lack of charity in a defensive aside:

> La fourmi n'est pas prêteuse :
> C'est là son moindre défaut.

> The ant is not a lender;
> This is her least fault.

Even greater discomfort appears in the work of La Fontaine's English near-contemporary, Sir Roger L'Estrange, a Royalist censor (known in his day as "the bloodhound of the Press") whose *Fables of Aesop and Other Eminent Mythologists: with Morals and Reflexions* (London, 1692) called fables the "Art of Schooling Mankind into Better Manners." Notwithstanding his determination to extract an edifying lesson from the fable of the ant and the grasshopper, he struggles to explain the ant's lack of charity, concluding, "The Ant did well to Reprove the Grasshopper for her Slothfulness; but she did Ill then to refuse her a Charity in her Distress." Nonetheless, the moral he extracts is unambiguous: "A Life of Sloth is the Life of a Brute; but Action and Industry is the Bus'ness of a Great, a Wise, and a Good Man."[30]

In 1818 Thomas Bewick adapts L'Estrange's version to arrive at a similar moral: "Action and industry is the business of a wise and a good man, and nothing is so much to be despised as slothfulness. Go to the Ant, thou sluggard, says the Royal Preacher, consider her ways, and be wise; which in a few words sums up the moral of this fable."[31] Conflating the Cynic's praise of *ponos* with the lesson of Proverbs 6:6-9 ("Go to the ant, you sluggard! Consider her ways and be wise, which having no captain, overseer or ruler, provides her supplies in the summer, and gathers her food in the harvest"), he gives the *vita activa* a biblical as well moral foundation: "action and industry" may be "the business of a wise and good man," but it is also the work of the Christian, provided one overlooks the ant's notably unChristian lack of charity.

Across its variations, the fable has challenged readers to find adequate themes and images for the unending conflict over *otium* and *negotium*, work and leisure, virtue and pleasure. One reason for its survival and constant revision is that these themes are central not only to the enduring question of the well-lived life but to the very function and purpose of the fable—and indeed, of art. Despite its warnings against the "foolish pastime," the fable is not against pastime per se: it can't be. It is itself an object of pastime, a piece of literature written to be consumed in leisure and, presumably, with pleasure. Apart from professional literary critics, no one who reads a fable performs an act of work. Yet the fable's challenge is to convince readers that fable-reading is a worthy pastime; in the process, it teaches readers how to approach it on two levels, insisting that what appears to be a light pleasure is in fact deeply useful.

Roger L'Estrange's edition opens with an image of Aesop holding a book bearing the words "Utile Dulci"—useful and pleasurable, the functions Horace attributed to literature in his *Ars Poetica*. Literature, the argument goes, achieves its utility through pleasure. So much more so with fables, which couch their moralizing lessons in compact, engaging forms. That pleasure advances utility is a point L'Estrange feels compelled to defend throughout his preface, railing against "a Certain set of Morose and Untractable Spirits in the World" who deem fables to be "only fit for Women and Children." These imagined opponents believe that philosophy must be harsh in order to be true, "as if a man could not be Wise and Honest, without being Inhumane: or, I might have said, without putting an Affront upon Christian Charity, Civil Society, Decency, and Good Manners."[32] To the contrary, L'Estrange insists, fables are both instructive and appealing. And with this, he identifies the source of his unease with "The Grasshopper and the Ants," which is, as he admits himself, "wise" in its lessons but "inhumane" in its delivery. With the ant's harshness to the starving grasshopper, the fable arguably fails to deliver on its central promise. Rather than achieving utility through pleasure, it tells us that pleasure kills and work saves. Rather than teaching moral lessons through pastime, it insists that the only path to virtue is to forgo leisure (even, potentially, fable-reading) and apply ourselves to painful toil.

. . .

The conflict between work and leisure, self-sufficiency and community, persisted into the twentieth century, when "The Grasshopper and the Ants" was adapted to the new medium of cinema and assumed the challenge of defining a new work ethic for an age of commodified leisure. The emergence of new forms of mass culture—radio, film, and popular magazines and paperbacks—redefined modern leisure, even as industrialization, the labor movement and labor standards, and the Depression redefined modern work. A growing division between work and leisure became institutionalized in new models of the workday and workweek. The nineteenth-century labor movement protested long workdays that allowed "never an hour for thought," and demanded instead "eight hours for work, eight hours for rest, eight hours for what we will," in the words of an anthem popularized by the so-called eight-hour-day movement.[33] But paradoxically, it was an industrialist, Henry Ford, who helped secure the forty-hour week. Believing that greater leisure would stimulate consumption and boost the economy, he closed his factories on Saturdays as well as the traditional Sundays and hoped that others would follow him. With the Depression in 1927, shorter work hours became a partial remedy for unemployment; individual workers would work less, but there would be more jobs for all.[34] But the reduction of working hours also stimulated new concerns about the dangers of idleness among the working classes. As labor historian E. P. Thompson observes, "The leisured classes began to discover the 'problem' ... of the leisure of the masses."[35]

Without long work hours to occupy them, the working classes

would be tempted into idleness and worse, worried journalists in the 1930s. Articles with titles like "The Bright Perilous Face of Leisure," "Out of Unemployment into Leisure," "Too Little Culture for Leisure," and "What Will We Do with Our Time?" raised the specter of idle workers falling into indolence because, unlike the traditional leisured classes, they had not been educated for its proper use.[36] In his 1934 book *The Challenge of Labor*, Arthur Pack advocated "the pursuit of constructive leisure," reassuring his readers that leisure could be socially beneficial if directed toward healthful and culturally enriching pursuits.[37] But others fretted that the siren call of popular culture would lead underemployed workers and youth to degeneracy.

Into this broad debate, the young Walt Disney studio introduced an animated adaptation of "The Grasshopper and the Ants" as part of its "Silly Symphony" series in 1934, testing the market and its own production methods before producing its first feature-length animation, *Snow White and the Seven Dwarfs*, in 1937. As "The Grasshopper and the Ants" opens, a fiddling grasshopper springs into view with a song (which would later become a hit, sung by Shirley Temple) that declares, "Oh, the world owes us a living!" Meanwhile, the hard-working ants toil to save food for the winter, only to be mocked by the grasshopper, who feeds off the leaves that grow abundantly in Disney's beautifully drawn, Technicolor setting. When winter comes and the leaves disappear, the grasshopper, emaciated and near-frozen, seeks shelter with the feasting ants. In a tone of reproach, the queen ant rises and declares, "Just those who work may stay, so take your fiddle"—there is a tense pause, and the grasshopper braces himself to be thrown out into the cold, until the queen completes the rhyme—"and play!" The queen's kindness to the grasshopper reverses the cruelty that troubled earlier readers of the fable. But she does not act out of charity, the film insists. Rather, she orders a calculated exchange that makes "play" a fungible product, a form of labor. The grasshopper, learning that his play can be a means of earning his keep, gratefully changes his tune: "I owe the world a living! I owe the world a living! I've been a fool the whole year long and now I'm singing a different song! You were right and I was wrong!" The animated short redeems the grasshopper's *otium* by placing it in the service of the ants' *negotium*.

The film thus responds to contemporary debates about the nature of leisure and work in America. Answering those who worried that excess leisure would lead to degeneracy, it insists that leisure can serve socially constructive purposes. Not only does the grasshopper learn to turn his leisure into labor that earns him compensation and entertains the hard-working ants, the film itself, like the fable before it, delivers an edifying, pro-work message through a leisure-time medium. *Dulce*, rendered *utile*, is redeemed.

This message about art transformed from idle and wasteful pleasure to productive industry was appropriate to Disney, a growing corporate power during the years of the Roosevelt New Deal. In 1934, shortly after the film's release, an article in *Fortune* hailed "The Grasshopper and the Ants" as a technical and artistic achievement as well as a moral one: "The Silly Symphony, as it attains the dignity of an institution, becomes increasingly a Force-for-Good."[38] Disney achieves this good through both his message and his method. His genius, the article observes, is to wed art and industry: "By a system as truly of the machine age as Henry Ford's plant at Dearborn, true art is produced."[39] "Disney has done his best to impose factory methods upon a craft which is essentially personal," to the point of making art on an assembly line, with workers "drawing innumerable little figures over and over again on paper and celluloid."[40] Disney's studio demonstrates the ultimate union of *dulce* and *utile*: as the article insists, it is "a factory for making myths."[41]

As Disney demonstrated at the dawn of American mass media culture, leisure had become big business. The time freed up by the forty-hour workweek and two-day weekend could be given over to consumption, channeled to generate and support new industries such as film. In the year of its release, "The Grasshopper and the Ants" was featured as a comic broadsheet published in *Good Housekeeping,* where it shared space with ads that recognized the growing power of wives as economic agents and households as centers of consumption. Most of the products featured in those ads catered to the growing market in self-care: the reader is advised to "Pour Yourself a Good Night's Sleep" with Absorbine, to "Prevent Humiliating Dishpan Hands" with Lux soaps, to "release your latent energy in a natural, harmless manner" with Camel cigarettes, and, mysteriously, to maintain "Marriage Hygiene" with Lysol.[42] Women bore special responsibility for the care of their families, as an ad for Vicks VapoRub confirms: "That Cold of Mine Was Awful . . . but Mom Knew What to Do for It!" Alongside such ads, "The Grasshopper and the Ants" in comic form presents its familiar narrative of redemption and salvation. As a rhyming caption proclaims, "He's learned his lesson: you must work and save, and never loaf or shirk." Just as consuming the right soaps and potions will restore physical health to individuals and families, the magazine promises, consuming the right leisure product— here, the Disney short as "Force-for-Good"—will restore moral health to society.

Disney not only creates art on an assembly line but depicts industrial efficiency in that art. As the *Fortune* author observes, "Disney is childishly enchanted by factory methods: they turn up constantly as a source of humor in his films."[43] This is much

FIGURE 2. Still from Disney's *The Grasshopper and the Ants*, 1934.

in evidence in "The Grasshopper and the Ants," whose opening scene features ants cheerfully but mechanistically process-
ing fruits and vegetables, sawing carrots into disks and prying
corn kernels from a cob, which they pass along a production line
to their winter stores. Even their feasting in the final scene re-
sembles the assembly line, as they rhythmically clink glasses,
pass dishes, and dance in rows to the grasshopper's new song. In
short, Disney's film extends the fable's effort to submit leisure
to work by creating a massively successful artistic industry that
both celebrates and exemplifies modern factory production. In
the process, it contributes to the ongoing debate over *otium* and
negotium by suggesting that leisure can support—and be thus
redeemed by—industrial capitalism, a lesson that leaves no
doubt about which wields the superior cultural power.

. . .

The 1960s recoiled from the assembly line–driven factory work that Disney celebrated, as well as the union of art and industry his films exemplified, regarding them as anathema to individual creativity and self-expression. This shift in understandings of work and leisure is reflected by new versions of the fable. In the Caldecott-winning children's book *Frederick* by Leo Lionni (1967), "The Grasshopper and the Ants" is retold as the story of a dreamy mouse who is unappreciated by his industrious brothers and sisters.

> "Frederick, why don't you work?" they asked.
> "I do work, said Frederick.
> "I gather sun rays for the cold dark winter days."

When the winter comes and the mice retreat to their den to live off their stores, Frederick comforts them with his poetry, and they in turn learn the value of his dreamy gifts. Like Disney's short, *Frederick* redeems art by insisting that it, too, counts as a form of "work"—but rather than transform art into productive industry, as Disney does, Frederick envisions it as part of a cultural ecosystem in which creative and industrious work create a harmonious balance. Frederick's poetry celebrates the order of nature, in which every season has its place: the summer "paints" the flowers, just as the industrious fall produces the harvest. Similarly, the seasons are "like you and I," Frederick observes unsubtly (and ungrammatically), insisting that we must appreciate society's dreamers, its meaning-makers, as well as its workers.

Lionni's *Frederick* validates Josef Pieper's thesis that leisure is "the basis of culture" by separating it from merely practical work but insisting on its equal value. The creative space of leisure, it invites us to conclude, is as important as work, however different the two might be. Yet, if *Frederick* attempts to redress the imbalance in prestige between leisure and work that is evident throughout the history of the "Grasshopper and the Ants" fable, it does nothing to challenge the polarization of the two terms. To the contrary, it perpetuates the split, as reflected in the book's reviews on Amazon.com. Supporting its gentle polemic in favor of creative leisure, one reviewer observes:

> The story of Frederick is simple. In a community narrowly focused on efficiency, one mouse stands apart and concerns himself with art. Frederick notes the wonder of the world he lives in, and takes the time to assimilate it. While his cohorts may grumble at this behavior, when the dreariness of winter overtakes them they are grateful for Frederick's words. Frederick's poetry is seen as an essential supply for survival.

But taking the earlier fable's line on work over idleness, another retorts:

> While the rest of the family was showing strong character and work ethic Frederick was a lazy day dreamer that made no contribution. If he had worked along side his family in preparation for winter they would have had more fuel for their bodies and straw to keep them warm. Essentially he became a burden on his family and could only share mystic thoughts of yesteryear while his siblings and parents starved themselves during the dead of winter.[44]

. . .

Taken together, the comments show how habitually we polarize the values of work and leisure, action and contemplation, however positive or negative the values we assign to each. Either *Frederick* "notes the wonder of the world," in opposition to the narrow efficiency of his community, or he is a "lazy day dreamer," in opposition to the "strong character and work ethic" of his family. In both cases, worker and dreamer define one another through their contrast: industry against nonproductivity, conformity against creativity. Missing from this vision is the possibility that one can pursue both creativity and productivity, utility and pleasure, personal fulfillment and material survival. If it rejects the commercial utopia of Disney's "Grasshopper and the Ants," which insists that art and work can become one, *Frederick* recuperates art only by cordoning it off from work, even while insisting on its value to the art-starved workers. The hard-working mice present a vision of workers as afflicted with "deep-rooted malaise" as the middle classes diagnosed by C. Wright Mills in 1951. If Frederick's poetry refreshes and distracts worker mice, it nonetheless confirms Mills's conclusion that "the faculties of reflection, imagination, dream, and desire, so far as they exist, do not now move in the sphere of concrete, practical work experience."[45] The best the workers can do is to create a space for the dreamer in their midst and allow themselves to enjoy the fruits of his inspiration.

· · ·

Questions about the place and relative values of labor and leisure, *negotium* and *otium*, have been debated, adapted, and transformed over successive generations; the long history of "The Grasshopper and the Ants" reflects and illuminates those questions and their changing treatment. Modern retellings of the tale expend their most energetic interpretive work insisting, against doubts raised in earlier versions, that the values of *negotium* are consistent with charity, and those of *otium* with a functioning society. Still, serious questions remain.

Is it possible to live a life both of utility and of pleasure, socially constructive work and personally regenerative leisure? Or must we sacrifice one to achieve the other? Is it possible to meet our personal needs while also serving the needs of our community? And if we work, who deserves our charity, our public support? Do artists? Today, these questions remain compelling, as they have been throughout the long history of "The Grasshopper and the Ants," and they continue to inflect the most recent version that we will examine. At the same time, changing conditions of work, leisure, and community have transformed many of the questions we ask and the answers that are available to us. What we mean today by these three terms—work, leisure, and community—may be radically different from their meanings in previous ages, as our networked lives defy past distinctions between work and nonwork, individuals and communities. Yet we continue to reach for the same myths in order to better understand and represent our experience, however dramatically we alter those myths in the process.

· · ·

When Pixar undertook its second animated feature in 1998, it followed the success of *Toy Story* (1995) with its own retelling of "The Grasshopper and the Ants." As with other Pixar films, this one started with a collaborative brainstorming session, which produced a novel take on both the fable itself and Disney's earlier version of it. In his history of Pixar, David A. Price reconstructs the scene: "In the Disney film, the Queen of the Ants kindly allows the grasshopper to earn his meal by fiddling for it. As [screenwriters Andrew] Stanton and [Joe] Ranft discussed the fable, they hit on the notion that the grasshopper, the larger insect by far, could just *take* the food."[46] By rebalancing the power between grasshopper and ants, Pixar's writers created an unconventional interpretation of the fable and the values of leisure and work that it had come to represent. In the process, they produced a new vision of work and its meanings for a networked generation.

The film's plot is easily summarized. In the opening scene, a colony of ants gathers food, though momentarily distracted by one of their company, Flik, an inventive misfit. But the ants have a bigger problem: every year, a portion of the grain they gather is given as an "offering" to a bullying cadre of grasshoppers. This year, Flik accidentally destroys the ants' offering, and the grasshoppers respond with an ultimatum: replenish the offering before winter or else. While the ants work desperately to meet the grasshoppers' demand, Flik travels off in search of bigger bugs who can fight the grasshoppers and liberate the ants. To the ants' surprise, he returns with a group of "warrior bugs," which turns out to be a troupe of down-on-their-luck circus performers. Nonetheless, when the grasshoppers return to claim their food, the ants and the circus bugs work together and fight off the oppressors through ingenuity and teamwork. As the film concludes, the grasshoppers are overthrown, and both the ants and the circus bugs recover their sense of community and purpose.

Where the Greek fable pits nonproductive leisure against productive labor, the central drama in Pixar's *Bug's Life* contrasts meaningless and meaningful work. Both the ant colony and the unsuccessful circus bugs are initially shown working without inspiration. The ants have been so fully subjugated to the grasshoppers that they cannot challenge the inequity of their situation, let alone diverge from their long-established routines. The circus bugs are similarly trapped by their work, their desperation to win audiences only leading them to danger, degradation, and burn-out (literally, as when the flea owner of the circus is incinerated in a stunt called "flaming death"). Both exemplify the dangers of working for others—the ants, for the tyrannical grasshoppers, and the circus bugs, for the audience that exploits and humiliates them. But together, the two groups of insects redeem one another: inspired by the circus bugs, the ants recover their sense of community ("Will you look at this colony!" exclaims its delighted princess while the ants party with the bugs), while through struggle, the circus bugs recover their sense of purpose (as one observes gratefully to Flik, "You have rekindled the long-dormant embers of purpose in our lives"). This message departs from earlier interpretations of the fable, not by recasting leisure in the service of industrial work, as in the 1930s Disney short, nor by making creative leisure and productive work separate but equal spheres, as did *Frederick* in the 1960s, but by showing work and leisure transformed by, and into, one another.

The medium of this reconciliation is Flik himself, who is marked from the beginning of the film as irredeemably different. When he tries to show off a harvesting machine he has invented, his fellow ants order him to "get back in line and pick grain like everybody else!" But Flik's inventiveness ultimately bridges the imagination of the circus bugs and the practicality of the ants, allowing the two communities to meet and transform one another. In this, Flik brings to mind the then-head of Pixar, Steve Jobs, whose career by the late 1990s was already transforming the meaning of work for a new generation. Despite his immense success as the founder of Apple, which made him an icon of Silicon Valley, Jobs situated himself "at the meeting place of technology and the humanities" and said he was drawn to Pixar because its culture brought together technology and creativity: "Silicon Valley folks don't really respect Hollywood creative types, and the Hollywood folks think that tech folks are people you hire and never have to meet," Jobs reflects in Walter Isaacson's posthumous biography. "Pixar was one place where both cultures were respected."[47] According to Brent Schlender, writing in *Fast Company*, Jobs's years at Pixar—coming after his bitter departure from Apple and before his fortuitous return— taught him how to direct creative talent and manage dynamic teams. In short, argues Schlender (breathlessly but not inaccurately), his time at Pixar "turned him into the kind of man, and leader, who would spur Apple to unimaginable heights upon his return."[48] As a story of two cultures, creative and practical, coming together to the benefit of both, *A Bug's Life* offers an organizational autobiography of Pixar at a moment of transition and of the new vision of work it would produce.

Flik is able to bridge two cultures because he's "different," proving that difference can be a positive value. Early in the film, he declares twice, "I just wanted to make a difference"— though both times in recognition of his failure to do so. But finally the ants are persuaded to follow Flik's lead, after their princess cajoles them ("I know it's not our tradition to do things differently") and they discover that they can come together in creativity and courage. Flik's ability to inspire the conformist ants to "do things differently"—and so "make a difference"— redefines "difference," from the stigma of the nonconformist to the source of collective transformation. This is the meaning of the word that surfaced at the center of Apple's well-known "think different" campaign, which coincided with Jobs's 1997 return:

Here's to the crazy ones. The misfits. The rebels. The troublemakers. The round pegs in the square holes. The ones who see things differently. They're not fond of rules. And they have no respect for the status quo. You can quote them, disagree with them, glorify or vilify them. About the only thing you can't do is ignore them. Because they change things. They push the human race forward. And while some may see them as the crazy ones, we see genius. Because the people who are crazy enough to think they can change the world, are the ones who do.

As an account of difference redeemed as the source of social transformation, the ad's celebration of misfits could be a treatment for *A Bug's Life*, then in final production and preparing for release the following year. Yet while the ad reflects the corporate mythology of Apple under the charismatic rule of Jobs, *A Bug's Life* envisions an alternative corporate model. Not simply the story of an individual misfit redeemed by genius, the film envisions a community redeemed through its ability to embrace genius and liberate itself from mindless conformity into collective creativity. According to screenwriter Andrew Stanton, the story challenges the conventional character-driven narrative: "We went in thinking that we had to do this very grand arc of Flik's character turning into something different. As I wrote it, I realized that it was about another dynamic. The main character didn't change, rather he changed the world of all the other characters in the story."[49] This might be the most unusual thing about *A Bug's Life*: its central drama doesn't concern an individual seeking redemption or self-fulfillment, but the redemption and fulfillment of a community with—literally—countless members.

For its makers, *A Bug's Life* involved considerably more work

FIGURE 3. Still from Pixar's *A Bug's Life*, 1998.

than its predecessor because the nature of the story demanded it: animating the ant colony meant creating a number of crowd scenes, and Pixar's artists were determined to render the ants individually, giving each ant its own look and character, rather than multiplying identical copies.[50] In the sequence that opens the film, a line of ants files along a translucent blade of grass, each carrying a grain, berry, or leaf. The sequence deliberately remakes the assembly line of ants in Disney's "Silly Symphonies" short, and it exemplifies the artistic challenge that the films' makers accepted: to create a story in which many distinct individuals would come together to form a community that experienced conflict, reintegration, and growth, the same arc of development undertaken by an individual character in a traditional drama.

The emphasis on community reflects the work culture of Pixar. "I work very differently from other screenwriters, because at Pixar I work as part of a group," observes Stanton. "It is a collaborative effort. The group is always there through the flow cycle to bounce ideas off."[51] From the outside perspective of the hierarchical corporate culture of Disney, which funded and shared billing for *A Bug's Life*, Pixar's collaborative ethos looked like disorganized chaos. According to Sarah McArthur, a Disney vice president who came to oversee production at Pixar during this period, "Everything was divided up between people. . . . There was nobody who had an oversight over the whole film."[52]

In contrast to freewheeling Pixar, Disney operated on a top-down model of authority. A 1999 *Fortune* magazine profile of Disney CEO Michael Eisner described "a corporate culture where decision-making is hierarchical, centralized, and slow. It's an utter mismatch for the Internet age."[53] The Disney corporate culture exacted a high price from its animators, who, according to James B. Stewart's *Disney War*, "were barely paid above scale" because the studio's leaders knew that they exercised a virtual monopoly: before Pixar and DreamWorks, there existed "almost no demand for their skills beyond Disney," which continued to require them to punch timecards.[54] As Jobs himself observed of Eisner, "Nobody liked working for him. They felt they had no authority. He had this strategic planning group that was like the Gestapo."[55] During the production of *A Bug's Life*, the relationship between Pixar and Disney was a contentious clash of cultures, with Disney treating Pixar like contract labor and Pixar bridling under its control.

The deeply entrenched differences between Disney's and Pixar's work cultures are reflected in the two companies' interpretations of "The Grasshopper and the Ants." Where the grasshopper in Disney's 1934 animated short became a model for the transformation of art into productive industry through discipline and authority, the grasshoppers in *A Bug's Life* have become industry bosses, whose exploitation drains workers of their creativity and agency. Once liberated from the oppressive grasshoppers, however, the ants are transformed from embattled drones of corporate hierarchy to a "dynamic network" of decentralized authority. This especially apt term belongs to Deborah Gordon, the Stanford biologist whose studies of ants have determined that "an ant colony operates without a central control or hierarchy, and no ant directs another."[56] Given their decentralized mode of work and living, ants were apposite models for the new, collaborative workplace Pixar strove to embody. The liberated ant colony of *A Bug's Life* exemplifies "the rise of the network society" that Manuel Castells associates with new models of work and identity in the information age. At a historical moment marked "by widespread destructuring of organizations, delegitimation of institutions, fading away of major social movements, and ephemeral cultural expressions," Castells finds, a "whole set of social relationships and social structures" is redefining individual identity and agency.[57] *A Bug's Life* offers a new fable for the network society, in which work and leisure come together in communities that are both creative and purposeful.

· · ·

Not only does *A Bug's Life* transform the concepts of work and leisure; it transforms the fundamental notions of action and contemplation that underlie them. Twentieth-century theorists of leisure identified it with the intellectual values of "ideas and imagination" (De Grazia) and "the faculties of reflection, imagination, dream, and desire," set apart from "the sphere of concrete, practical work experience" (Mills).[58] Such definitions are consistent with those of medieval thinkers, who believed imagination to be the first stage of contemplation. As medievalist Michelle Karnes has shown, the faculty of imagination was taken extremely seriously in the Middle Ages as a form of heightened cognition, a path to superrational understanding that could lead to the highest levels of wisdom.[59] The very term "idea" betrays its Platonic origins, coming to us directly from Plato's Greek. For Plato, "idea" is an image that exists in the mind, distinct from matter, representing an eternal truth or abstract form reached through contemplation.

Contrast this contemplative "idea" with the term's appearance in *A Bug's Life*. Flik first appears in the film wielding one of his inventions, announcing happily, "This is my new idea for harvesting grain!" "Idea" here is synonymous with "invention," The same use occurs later in the film, when Flik takes responsibility for a contraption the ants and the bugs have constructed to frighten the grasshoppers, a giant mechanical bird. Flik declares, "The bird was my idea!" Again, the "idea" doesn't precede but coincides with the act of invention: it is abstract thought made material. It isn't simply that ideas *have* consequences. Ideas *are* consequences, the place where abstract contemplation and material action come together. This is the place that the film associates with freedom. By contrast, the grasshoppers insist, "Ideas are very dangerous things. You are mindless, soil-shoving losers, put on this earth to serve us!" The drudgery of the ants toiling under the grasshoppers is "mindless," while meaningful work produces "ideas."

At the film's end, Flik's grain harvester, which marks him as a misfit at the beginning of the film, has been adopted by the reformed ant community, which uses it not just for work but for fun: in the final shots, the ants fire stalks of grain into the air, which explode like fireworks. In this, *A Bug's Life* replaces the meaningless work of the ants' former drudgery with the capacity for play. Unlike the Disney's 1934 "Grasshopper and the Ants," in which "play" was transformed into remunerative work, play in *A Bug's Life* infuses community and work with transformative creative energy.

Play, as Thomas Aquinas insisted, is comparable to contemplative wisdom, since both are activities undertaken for their own sake and for no other instrumental purposes. "Play is delightful, and the contemplation of wisdom brings the greatest joy," he observes, noting that just as "sports are not means to ends but are sought for their own sake, so also are the delights of wisdom."[60] Strikingly, though, the long history of "The Grasshopper and the Ants" associates this kind of non-instrumental play with the grasshopper, not the ants. Indeed, a much-admired book by philosopher Bernard Suits, *The Grasshopper: Games, Life and Utopia*, takes the fable's grasshopper to embody the very principle of "play," defined as "any intrinsically valuable activity," which Suits calls "the ideal of existence."[61]

By assigning play to its ants, rather than its grasshoppers (who are merely lazy brutes), *A Bug's Life* collapses the opposition between work and play, *otium* and *negotium*, that has driven generations of retellings and interpretations of "The Grasshopper and the Ants." Instead, the film offers up a conception of work that embraces, rather than excluding, the concept of play. As educators have long known, play is a necessary part of learning and cognitive development—and, in a message now popularized by business analysts, it can also be a catalyst for creativity and innovation in the workplace. This is the kind of creative "work" that *A Bug's Life* imagines. In the process, it makes a case for film itself as a model of a new kind of creative work. Its protagonist's name, Flik, is, after all, vernacular for "film." In this model workplace, play isn't separated from work itself, though it is the opposite and enemy of the meaningless drudgery the ants experience under the tyrannical control of the grasshoppers, who deny them even the power to think. If play is a form of wisdom, to recall Aquinas, it brings work closer to a state of contemplation envisioned by the original meaning of leisure as *otium*—not mindless recreation, as it came to mean in the twentieth century, but the experience of intrinsically meaningful, deeply engaged reflection and cognitive expansion.

. . .

Our students grew up with *A Bug's Life*, and they resonated with its vision of work and leisure as not diametrically opposed but mutually enriching. Like the film's makers, they hoped to find work that embodied deep creativity and meaning as well as connection within community; they hoped, like its ant protagonist, "to make a difference." They are, after all, the generation that told the UCLA survey they wished "to develop a meaningful philosophy of life" as well as to achieve material comfort, to "help others in difficulty" as well as to write, create, and perform in the arts. These goals do not cancel one another out, but they do demand a more expansive vision of how work, life, and meaning can come together.

What will it take for them to realize these goals? They are fortunate to live in a place and time in which meaningful work can be a valid aspiration—and one not restricted to the graduates of selective universities. However, our age also exploits that aspiration: it is commonplace to exhort young people to find work about which they can be passionate. But "finding your passion" can too easily translate into selfish myopia, a drive toward individual career success rather than authentic contribution. Even the deep, meaning-seeking work of contemplation, as we have seen, can be offered (and corporately sponsored) in the interests of the bottom line.

At our transitional moment we can find fresh relevance in Schumacher's call for "good work" or Aristotle's for "being-at-work in accord with virtue." But it will take more than a motivational article or a meditation class during lunch to find the meaningful work that Schumacher and Aristotle invoke and our students seek. It will also take an expanded notion of higher education. While many today decry the "careerism" that pervades higher education and threatens to reduce it to no more than workforce training, good work is, as Schumacher reminds us, aligned with education's highest purpose:

> Education for good work could . . . begin with a systematic study of traditional wisdom, where answers are to be found to the questions What is man? Where does he come from? What is the purpose of his life? It would then emerge that there is indeed a goal to be reached and that there is also a path to the goal—in fact, that there are many paths to the same summit. . . . In short, life is some sort of school, and in this school nothing counts but good work, work that ennobles the product as it ennobles the producer.[62]

As Shumacher can remind us—including the cynical interpreters of the UCLA survey of freshmen—finding good work such as this doesn't foreclose the search for a meaningful philosophy of life. It fulfills it.

· 5 ·

Public and Private

In October 2014 an unlikely book entered the *New York Times* bestseller list. The immense popularity of Marie Kondō's *The Life-Changing Magic of Tidying Up* surprised everyone— especially its editors, who hardly expected that a book about cleaning would reach beyond a niche market. Yet the small book sold more than two million copies, remaining—a year later—at the top of the *Times*' "Advice, How-To & Miscellaneous" list. Its author was even named one of *Time* magazine's 100 Most Influential People.

As its title suggests, *The Life-Changing Magic of Tidying Up* is about more than housecleaning. To its readers, frequently referred to as "cultlike," it has a quasi-religious appeal. One reviewer calls it "a mystical manifesto." Another remarks on the book's "almost religious emphasis on the virtues of purity and order."[1] Kondō encourages the association, citing testimony from a client: "Tidying has far more effect than feng shui or power stones or other spiritual goods." The very act of tidying is a "sacred act."[2] When she first enters a client's house, Kondō kneels on the floor, addresses the house in a silent prayer, and asks it to assist her. Though unorthodox, she observes, "I began this custom quite naturally based on the etiquette of worshipping at Shinto shrines."[3] As a young woman, Kondō served for five years as a *Miko*, or shrine maiden, at such a shrine, where her duties included the performance of purification rituals. "At a shrine, there is an air of purity, cleanliness and calm," she observes in an interview. "That's the kind of atmosphere I feel after decluttering a room."[4] Tidying, she insists, "is really about examining your inner self, a rite of passage to a new life."[5]

The desire for a clean house often expresses itself as a spiritual calling—or perhaps the reverse is true. Sue Bender's *Plain and Simple: A Woman's Journey to the Amish*—a 1989 publisher's phenomenon—recounts its author's effort to restore meaning to a distracted life by sojourning with an Amish community in Ohio. While deeply personal, even idiosyncratic, the small book resonated at the end of the decade that gave us the term "workaholic." By speaking out on behalf of stillness and depth amid the clamor of contemporary life, Bender launched the "simplicity movement," clearing the way for Kondō's rapturous reception. Bender reports being drawn to the Amish, whose lives of simplicity and calm offered her a new ideal; after staying with several Amish families, she discovers the rewards of slowing down, that "beneath all the frenzy was the very thing, that inner calm I was seeking."[6] Resolving to bring this discovery back to her harried Californian life, she redecorates her kitchen in an uncluttered, calming white and, following the example of her Amish hosts, learns to experience joy in the everyday tasks of cleaning and cooking: "I cleaned my house, bought plants, got cookbooks out of the library, and slowed down my usual incessant workpace." Eventually, she writes, "The state of mind I had when I was with the Amish is with me in my kitchen."[7]

Plain and Simple launched not only a vogue for Amish crafts but a new domestic idiom. Writing in 2013, Emily Matchar calls it "the New Domesticity" and analyzes its appeal to burned-out working women who seek fulfillment and quasi-spiritual redemption in housework.[8] The phenomenon has sparked feminist debate about whether it betrays the gains professional women made in the preceding decades, by encouraging them to turn their attention from the public sphere of work toward the traditionally female, private sphere of the home. It's worth pausing here to define and understand "public" and "private." The terms are complex and porous—particularly as applied to women—and are inevitably bound up with ideas about the active and the contemplative life. Not only do they assign "active" and "contemplative" to distinct locales, distinguishing the tumult of the marketplace and political arena from the calm and inwardness of the home or monastic cell; by separating the "public" world of men from the "private" world of women, they also assign action and contemplation different genders.

The association of the public arena with men and the private with women is underwritten by the terms that continue to define them. *Pubes*, the root of "public," means post-adolescent males, while *privatus*, the root of "private," signifies children, women, and slaves—those who are "deprived" of the public privileges of masculinity. Given this etymology and the long history it represents, it is easy to assume that these associations—of women with the private sphere of the home and men with the public sphere of work and politics—are innate, the genetic legacy of our hunter-gatherer ancestors or the result of divine decree. As Matchar puts it, the "twenty-first-century veneration for all things 'natural'" can also naturalize women's exclusion from the workforce amid "praise for women's 'primal' nurturing instinct and for women's 'natural' ability and desire to care for the home."[9]

Yet these sexual divisions of public and private are more ideological than natural, and they tend to be reinforced at historical moments that seek to limit women's economic and political (that is, public) influence by insisting that their natural or God-given place is in the home. Those who study the history of domesticity remind us that the "privacy" of the domestic sphere, imagined as a place set apart and protected from the "public" realm of politics, society, and economics, has only ever been illusory. Indeed, for Greeks, the home, or *oikos*, formed the basic building block (and etymological root) of the "economy," as a primary place of consumption as well as production and distribution.[10] Today, economists have reminded us that "home" is imaginable as the opposite of "work" only if we render invisible the many forms of labor that take place inside it, whether performed by servants or by a "housewife" (despite claims—her own or others'—that she doesn't "work"). It is a place of production as well as consumption, myriad forms of activity as well as rest. The idea of the home as a female refuge set apart from work and the world is always a fiction—which is why it must be retold again and again.

Yet the aim of domestic authors such as Kondō or Bender isn't to promote a retreat into the home but to repair the imbalances of late capitalism. For Kondō, that imbalance is evident in the mindless accumulation of things; for Bender, it is "addiction to activity." Yet their solutions are not to eliminate things or activity but to redeem them. Kondō traces the nascence of her book to an epiphany following a near breakdown. After a frenzy of throwing things away, she is awakened into a new consciousness by "a mysterious voice, like some god of tidying telling me to look at my things more closely." She realizes that things are not the problem; indeed, she needs to preserve those that "spark joy." "Identifying the things that make you happy: that is the work of tidying."[11] Bender reports similarly that in the Amish houses she visited she found not an absence of activity but activities endowed with near sacred meaning: "What I saw among the Amish was the amazing amount of energy available to people who get pleasure from what they are doing and find meaning in the work itself . . . For them it's all connected."[12] Home, in other words, isn't a haven from work but a place that brings everyday work and transcendent meaning together into an integrated whole. Home is the place that models the transformative potential of "meaning in the work," rather than insisting on the separation of meaning and work. In contrast to the fragmentation she experienced in her own life, she observes that the Amish lead lives of wholeness: "No distinction was made between the sacred and the everyday." "Their life was all one piece. It was all sacred—and all ordinary."[13]

To the extent that we continue to associate the *vita contemplativa* with formal religious practice—and to many, the association remains implicit, if not vital—we might be tempted to link the rise of the active life and the apparent eclipse of the contemplative with the dominance of secular values in modern society. The historical narrative would run like this: when it became possible to speak of "church" and "state" as distinct entities, when monasticism, whether western or eastern, ceased to be a common career choice, then the very possibility of a *vita contemplativa* was pushed to the social margins, along with the formal religious frameworks to which it had once been central. Contemplation, along with religious devotion, became a private pursuit—one that answered personal needs rather than widespread social or political ones—and thus disappeared from public view. The longing that Bender and others identify speaks to a deeper need that remains following the ebb of formal, shared religious experience. Many secular practices offer to fill that need, from yoga to interior decoration, but we move hungrily from one item to the next in our culture's spiritual buffet, deprived of the divine food we crave. This is one version of the story of religion and modernity. But there is another.

Until very recently, the idea that we live in a secular age went almost unchallenged. But a resurgence of public discussion of religion—whether led by the vocal "new atheists" or religious apologists from myriad denominations—calls this observation into question, suggesting that it is time to rethink what we mean by secularity, its so-called rise, and its apparent hold over the public arena. One of the most articulate and thoughtful participants in this discussion has been Charles Taylor, professor emeritus of philosophy at McGill University and author of *A Secular Age* (2007). Defining secularism as a frame of reference in which "public spaces" are "emptied of God," Taylor insists that secularism's triumph has been less thorough or ineluctable than it appears. While this thesis might be supported by the majority of North Americans who claim religious belief, or by the highly visible role of religion in US politics, Taylor finds deeper, more subtle evidence for his argument in apparently secular institutions and practices. Within a dominant commercial culture professing values that are largely material and individualistic, Taylor identifies a mounting critique. A perception "that the modern world lacked depth, and the modern self, wholeness," is countered by widespread longing for an experience of "integrity or generosity or abandonment or self-forgetfulness."[14] Rather than directing this search toward traditional religious institutions, today's seekers are drawn to what Taylor calls a "sanctification of ordinary life," which finds evidence of the sacred not in the church and clergy but in direct lived experiences.[15] According to Taylor, the secularization of the public sphere has led not to the privatization, social marginalization, or disappearance of the holy, but to its dispersal, and even multiplication.

Taylor's thesis frames in a religious context our contention that the *vita activa* and the *vita contemplativa* are not only still vital, but interrelated and interdependent. This is particularly true if we consider contemplative values, like Taylor's search for the holy, to be dispersed throughout a wide range of apparently secular practices and places. One of those places is the home. The home has long borne a privileged relation to contemplative practice, particularly in historical contexts that have defined it against the public spheres of workplace and marketplace. Thomas à Kempis's *The Imitation of Christ*, which has remained a Christian devotional staple from the fifteenth century to the present, counsels its reader "to stay at home" and "seek a suitable time for leisure and meditate often on the favors of God," observing, "Anyone, then, who aims to live the inner and spiritual life must go apart, with Jesus, from the crowd."[16] The idea of the home as a personal sanctuary from the impious crowd was elevated to a cult in the nineteenth century, when domestic home design emphasized privacy and enshrined the "angel in the house," the middle-class wife and mother whose isolation from work and commerce made her the spiritual anchor of her family.

Our age is also witnessing a powerful movement to redefine the home in relation to the marketplace, not by setting the home apart from work and market, as it was in the nineteenth and twentieth centuries, but by accepting the direct relationship between home and market, and making it an object of special attention. By reclaiming the home as *oikos*—the elementary unit of economy, work, and socialization—some contemporary homemakers are reinventing domesticity as a place where the public and the private, the global and the individual, even the active and the contemplative, intermingle and animate one another. In the process, they make the household into a locus of what Taylor terms the "sanctification of ordinary life," a place where everyday activity carries the potential of holiness—not as sanctuary from the outside world but as *microcosm* modeling an ordered world. If the nineteenth- and twentieth-century home upheld a model of separate spheres, the contemporary home, we propose, offers a model of integration. And that integration—the meeting of public and private, where cosmos becomes microcosm—is what makes the home a sacred space, a place of what Taylor calls "fullness" instead of fragmentation.

· · ·

For Plato, Aristotle, and Cicero, the concepts of *theoria* and *praxis* were modeled on the occupations of men—statesman and philosopher, soldier and scholar, all positions from which women were excluded. But when *theoria* and *praxis* entered the Hebrew and Christian Bible, they did so in relation to work specific to women in the home. The biblical representatives of "action" and "contemplation" are two pairs of sisters: Leah and Rachel in the Old Testament, and Mary and Martha in the New. For both rabbinical and patristic commentators, their stories allowed the classical debate to be adapted to and made meaningful within a Judeo-Christian religious framework. The stories are similar to the extent that both feature loving rivalries between sisters, and they came to symbolize the devout life for both Jews and Christians who read and interpreted them. Most significantly, they asked the devout of both genders to identify with female exemplars.

The story of Rachel and Leah cuts across several chapters of Genesis but can be summarized briefly: Jacob is commanded by his father, Isaac, to "take a wife for yourself from among the daughters of Laban, your mother's brother" (28:2). Laban has two daughters, of whom we learn, "Leah had weak eyes, but Rachel was lovely in form, and beautiful" (29:17). Jacob falls in love with Rachel and agrees to work under Laban for seven years for her hand. Having done so, however, he is tricked, waking the morning after his wedding to find he has married Leah. Jacob labors for another seven years and is finally granted Rachel as his second wife, "and he loved Rachel more than Leah" (29:30). In recompense, "when the Lord saw that Leah was not loved, he opened her womb, but Rachel was barren" (29:21). After Leah bears Jacob many sons, Rachel finally becomes pregnant and dies giving birth to her second son, Benjamin (35:18).

The first commentators read Leah and Rachel as allegories of human knowing and doing. Philo of Alexandria (also known as Philo the Jew) insisted that weak-eyed Leah represents the highest part of reason, "which yearns to see and learn," while the merely beautiful Rachel represents the lower, worldly forms of experience: "Since our soul is twofold, with one part reasoning and the other unreasoning, each has its own virtue or excellence, the reasoning Leah, the unreasoning Rachel."[17] To Philo, the fruitful Leah represents one who is filled with "the seed of wisdom" and thereby "brings forth beautiful ideas worthy of the Father who begat them." He thus urges readers to "follow Leah's example and turn away from mortal things."[18]

Later rabbinical commentators accepted Philo's categories but reversed their assignment to the two sisters. In Midrash, the beautiful yet barren Rachel becomes a prophetess. The rivalry between Rachel and Leah represents the conflict between love and motherhood, the transcendent and the worldly.[19] This interpretation carried over in Christian interpretations of the two sisters. Saint Augustine insisted that the weak-eyed but fruitful Leah represents "the toils and hazards of an active life," while Rachel represents "the life devoted to contemplation," which seeks "to see with no feeble mental eye things invisible to flesh ... and to discern the ineffable manifestation of the eternal power and divinity of God, seeks leisure from all occupation, and is therefore barren."[20] The interpretation persisted through the Middle Ages and beyond. In Dante's *Purgatorio*, the two sisters pursue occupations that reflect their status as representatives of the active and contemplative lives, "labor" and "seeing." Leah makes flower garlands, while Rachel contemplates her own beauty in a mirror:

> "Whoever asks my name, know that I'm Leah,
> and I apply my lovely hands to fashion
> a garland of the flowers I have gathered.
> To find delight within this mirror I
> adorn myself; whereas my sister Rachel
> never deserts her mirror; there she sits
> all day; she longs to see her fair eyes gazing,
> as I, to see my hands adorning, long:
> she is content with seeing, I with labor." (27.100–108)

In the New Testament, Leah and Rachel were seen to prefigure another pair of sisters, Mary and Martha, whose story, which appears in the book of Luke, is short enough to quote in full:

Now it came to pass, as they were on their journey, that he entered into a certain village: and a woman named Martha welcomed him into her house. And she had a sister called Mary, who also seated herself at the Lord's feet, and listened to his word. But Martha was busy about much serving. And she came up and said, "Lord, is it no concern of thine that my sister has left me to serve alone? Tell her therefore to help me." But the Lord answered and said to her, "Martha, Martha, thou art anxious and troubled about many things: And yet only one thing is needful. Mary hath chosen the best part, and it will not be taken away from her."[21]

In the earliest interpretations of this episode, Martha stands for the *vita activa*. "Busy about much serving" and "anxious and troubled about many things," she leads a worthy life. But Mary, whose attentiveness to Jesus's words represents the "one thing" that is "needful," "hath chosen the best part," the *vita contemplativa* to which all Christians should aspire.

Notwithstanding the priority of contemplation over action, medieval theologians tended to stress the close relation between the two. "In these two women," remarks Augustine, "the two lives are figured, the life present, and the life to come, the life of labor, and the life of quiet, the life of sorrow, and the life of blessedness, the life temporal, and the life eternal."[22] Augustine builds this distinction between worthy labor and worthier quiet on the sisters' occupations as reported by Luke: Mary listens, and Martha serves (Luke's term for Martha's work is *diakonia*, which literally means "table-service," but not necessarily meal preparation: in a Eucharistic context, it could also mean preparation for worship, which is why medieval priests and abbots identified with the life of Martha).[23] Nonetheless, Augustine stresses that the two women are united in their kinship as sisters. Likewise, Origen insists on the essential unity of Martha and Mary. "You might reasonably like Martha to stand for action and Mary for contemplation," he writes. Nonetheless, they represent two sides of the Christian life: "For there is no action without contemplation, or contemplation without action."[24]

FIGURE 4. Diego Velázquez, *Christ in the House of Martha and Mary*, 1618.
Oil on canvas, 60 × 103.5 cm. Bequeathed by Sir William H. Gregory, 1892.
Photograph © National Gallery, London/Art Resource, New York.

With Mary and Martha, as with Leah and Rachel, action and contemplation are close relatives. Like their Old Testament counterparts, their home becomes a site of both tension and intimacy between contrasting attributes. The domestic, in both cases, is not a place of contemplation at the expense of action, or action at the expense of contemplation, but one where action and contemplation are brought together in dynamic but loving equipoise.

Martha and Mary became a favorite subject for artists in the later Renaissance, and their paintings reflect changing views of the two sisters. Where medieval theologians stress the sisters' kinship, Renaissance artists depict a growing sense of conflict. One of the best known of these paintings is *Christ in the House of Martha and Mary* (1618), by Diego Velázquez, which places the scene of Martha and Mary in the background, seen over the shoulder of a servant girl, who is laboring to prepare a meal. While the servant girl is not mentioned in Luke, her very presence in the painting—and location in the foreground—invites us to reconsider the "two lives" of Martha and Mary. As Christ directs Martha to honor Mary's "better choice"—his speech indicated by his hand gesture—the servant girl reminds us that meals must still be made, and made by those who have no option to favor the contemplative life over the active. The message is underscored by the old woman at the servant girl's side: her raised finger echoes Christ's gesture, but her message, reminding the unhappy girl of her kitchen duty, is the opposite.

Velázquez accentuates the contrast between the worldly scene of food preparation and the inset scene of divine instruction in their contrasting scale, which suggests that they occupy two different—and literally distant—worlds. This theme would be taken up in later paintings of Martha and Mary, which emphasize the differences between the two sisters and reflect a growing sense that the life of worldly business and that of speculative reflection are at odds. In Dutch painter Pieter de Bloot's *Christ in the House of Mary and Martha* (1637), Mary sits with Christ, bathed in light and poring over a book (judging by its size most likely a Bible), while Martha gestures toward a table in the foreground (as in Velázquez, laden with foodstuffs), in an attempt to compel her sister's attention from the eternal to the temporal, from the word of God to the stuff of life.

The foregrounded world of Martha recalls the visual conventions of the still life, an artistic staple in the Dutch Golden Age. Through lavish displays of perishable goods, the genre celebrated the low countries' commercial success.[25] Paintings like de Bloot's, which portray Mary and Martha alongside the overabundant still life, troubled some contemporaries. The Italian religious painter Vincente Carducho charged them with portraying "such an assortment of food, of mutton, capons, turkeys, fruit, dishes and other kitchen utensils" that they make Martha's house appear "more like a tavern of gluttony than a hospice of piety and careful restraint."[26] The description rings true for a painting like Frans Ykens's *Martha and Mary*, in which the biblical scene, miniaturized in the background, is nearly overwhelmed by the meats, fruit, flowers, and dead game that crowd the foreground.

Such paintings challenge viewers to consider how, or whether, material prosperity and personal piety can be reconciled, a challenge that commercial success made urgent for the mercantile Dutch. Whether the paintings stress conflict, as some art historians insist, or propose (as others hold) an expansive perspective that embraces both piety and worldliness, it is important to point out that they do not set the housewife Martha apart from the world of commerce and marketplace but, to the contrary, cast her as its representative.[27] The mercantile Dutch, in other words, are invited to see themselves and their dilemma

FIGURE 5. Pieter de Bloot, *Christ with Mary and Martha*, 1637.
Oil on panel, 47 × 66 cm. Liechtenstein Museum, Vienna.

FIGURE 6. Frans Ykens, *Christ in the House of Martha and Mary,*
seventeenth century. Private collection. Photograph: Roy Miles
Fine Paintings/Bridgeman Images.

reflected back to them in the figure of Martha and her material
world. As a representative of the commercial world, this late
Renaissance housewife gives the lie to the sexual divisions of
"public" and "private" adopted by later modernity. Rather than
serving as a refuge from the public world, Martha's house is a
place where public and private meet in conflict. Where Martha
brings the outside world in, Mary shows that inwardness is
not intrinsic to the household space but a pursuit that must be
learned, cultivated, and carefully guarded.

· · ·

Today's interpretations of Martha and Mary resemble those of
the Middle Ages, with their emphasis on the sisters' kinship,
more than the conflict-ridden versions of later periods. A. S.
Byatt's short story "Christ in the House of Martha and Mary"

(1998) focuses on Velázquez's servant girl, who converses with the unseen painter, who in turn endows her with the same contemplative gifts as Mary: "The Church teaches that Mary is the contemplative life, which is higher than Martha's way, which is the active way. But any painter must question, which is which? And a cook also contemplates mysteries."[28]

Martha's redemption in spiritually sanctioned housework features also in recent books addressed to Christian women. The Christian best-seller *Having a Mary Heart in a Martha World*, by Joanna Weaver (first published in 2000), instructs its readers on how to find "intimacy with God in the busyness of life." Similarly, *31 Days to Clean: Having a Martha House the Mary Way*, by Sarah Mae (2011), posits spiritual value in housework. Perhaps unintentionally, books such as these draw on a long religious tradition of sacred housework: Meister Eckhart, commenting on the scriptural passage "the good housewife looks well to the ways of her house, not eating the bread of idleness," insists that "this house represents the soul as a whole, and the ways of the house are the powers of the soul."[29] Where Meister Eckhart envisions housework allegorically, Saint Teresa of Avila means it literally when she counsels nuns, "Let there be no disappointment when obedience keeps you busy in outward tasks. If it sends you to the kitchen, remember that the Lord walks among the pots and pans and that He will help you in inward tasks and in outward ones too."[30] In the form of the contemplative cook or the Christian homemaker, Martha materializes contemplation by bringing it home.

. . .

The same spiritualization of the home informs contemporary treatments of the Jewish Shabbat. Sabbath observance, insists

Judith Shulevitz's *The Sabbath World: Glimpses of a Different Order of Time* (2010), has the power "to turn the ordinary into the singular. A weekly house scrubbing, when done on Friday, becomes a way of making one's home ready for God. A dinner party for family and neighbors attains the status of a royal banquet."[31] Shabbat is both a rest from housework and a celebration of it: "One day a week it honors the homes [that Jewish] wives make, the nourishment they provide, the bodies with which they make more bodies."[32] "The soul cannot celebrate alone," writes Abraham Joshua Heschel in *The Sabbath*, "so the body must be invited to partake in rejoicing of the Sabbath."[33] This integration of body and spirit echoes the classical Jewish philosopher Philo, who explains and defends the Sabbath observance to the Romans in the language of *theoria* and *praxis*: in the Sabbath, he emphasizes, "the best forms of life, the theoretical and the practical, take their turn in replacing each other."[34] Philo employs similar terms in his discussion of Rachel and Leah: just as the sisters represent the twofold soul, so the days of rest and work combine to represent "the best forms of life." The Sabbath sanctifies the dynamic balance of action and contemplation, and locates that balance in the home.[35]

· · ·

The home that emerges in these more recent versions challenges the strict divide between public and private, workplace and sanctuary, that circumscribed it under the mercantile capitalism of the Dutch Golden Age or the industrial capitalism of the Victorians, and rejects the Cartesian dualism that ruled those earlier eras. Where Heschel claims the Sabbath as "a day of the soul as well as the body," Kondō's purified houses abound with spirit-infused things.[36] Shinto *kami* (sacred spirits) reside in animals and plants as well as sanctified objects (*yori-shiro*) such as stones, swords, or trees. Likewise, Kondō endows household objects with vitality that is affronted by disorder. Socks, when folded carefully, breathe "a sigh of relief," while purses and shoes earn expressions of gratitude at the end of a hard-working day. Even objects that are thrown out are ensouled: "Free them from the prison to which you have relegated them. Help them leave that deserted isle to which you have exiled them. Let them go, with gratitude. Not only you, but your things as well, will feel clear and refreshed when you are done tidying."[37]

Such a reverence for things, like the Shinto religion from which it draws, reflects an animistic worldview that once perplexed Western observers. Supposing dualism to be the hallmark of cultural and religious maturity, religious historian Edward Burnett Tyler, writing in 1871, ascribes animism to "tribes very low in the scale of humanity."[38] "He who recollects when there was still personality to him in posts and sticks, chairs and toys, may well understand how the infant philosophy of mankind could extend the notion of vitality to what modern science only recognizes as lifeless things."[39] Countering this view, Kondō animates "lifeless things" and in the process invents a new domestic sacrality for the post-capitalist age.

· · ·

With its advocacy of the local and handmade against the environmental and global depredations of industrial agriculture, the locavore movement makes the home into a secular temple. The rise of cheese making, beekeeping, front-yard gardening, and an anticommercial DIY ethic offer evidence of a new suburban georgic. The locavore movement may have many parents, but its laureate is Barbara Kingsolver, whose *Animal, Vegetable, Miracle: A Year of Food Life* (2007) recounts "the story of a year in which [her family] made every attempt to feed ourselves animals and vegetables whose provenance we really knew . . . and of how our family was changed by our first year of deliberately eating food produced from the same place where we worked, went to school, loved our neighbors, drank the water, and breathed the air."[40] Though it slips in almost imperceptibly, the book's premise is grounded in the first message of the Gospel, the Golden Rule. The religiosity of *Animal, Vegetable, Miracle* is so subtle it feels like the book's unconscious. In interviews, Kingsolver claims to be a "pantheist," but she returns frequently enough to biblical language and themes to beg interpretation—and to suggest that her Sabbath of food will offer a theology for a newly sacralized domesticity.

When *Animal, Vegetable, Miracle* discusses agriculture and food, it veers frequently into an unexpectedly penitential language of atonement and redemption. "The conspicuous consumption of limited resources has yet to be accepted widely as a spiritual error," the book observes, promising that it will remedy this silence and expose the spiritual side of our consumerist fall from grace.[41] As Kingsolver's sabbatarian language suggests, she is proposing not only a new way of eating but a new underlying spirituality and cosmology. Yet rather than speaking as a minister, she sets herself up as a heretic; she admits to being a recusant from "the religion of time-saving," which drives its followers "to zip through a meal or a chore, rushing everybody out the door to the next point on a schedule."[42] Likewise, she professes to violate what she calls the popular religion of "overwork . . . whose holy trinity is efficiency, productivity, and material acquisition. Complaining about it is the modern equivalent of public prayer."[43]

Having rejected the orthodoxy of productivity, which appears to commodify people as much as it does the industrial food they consume, Kingsolver resists the countertemptation of leisure, the traditional antidote to relentless work. To the contrary, she admits to a Martha-like addiction to work, calling herself "a dweeby ant in a grasshopper nation." Far from prescribing relaxation or rest, she insists that the only effective cure for American overwork is active meditation: "It could be tennis or birdwatching. So long as it's meditative and makes you feel better afterward. Growing sunflowers and beans is like that, for some of us. Cooking is like that."[44] Such meditative activity also assumes an implicitly religious savor. Following their conversion from the worship of "efficiency, productivity, and material acquisition," Kingsolver calls the members of her family "pilgrims of a secret order" and observes that "tradition, vows, something *like* religion was working for us now, in our search for a new way to eat."[45] Something *like* religion. In lieu of a traditional deity, Kingsolver professes a new devotion to what she calls Creation: "In my household credo, Thanksgiving is Creation's birthday party. Praise harvest, a pause and sigh on the breath of immortality."[46]

In *A Secular Age*, Charles Taylor notes that "the search for spiritual wholeness is often closely related to the search for health."[47] This might be justly observed of many locavore practitioners, whether they are explicitly religious or (more likely) not. But what is striking about Kingsolver's into-the-wilderness narrative is how little interest she expresses in physical health (among all the good results the family's locavore experiment accomplished, she reports in the end, losing weight was not one). Instead, she professes interest in the health of the planet and sees food as the conduit from the microcosmic to the cosmic. In an interview she explains her driving commitment: "So many different issues come back to roost in our refrigerators or on our pantry shelves. The way we eat determines how we use the world." Food is a manifestation of our symbiotic relationship with the world, a reminder that "all living systems are connected." Thus, she explains, she led her family to undertake its "food sabbatical" to affirm this connection, "to reengage both as a mental exercise and a spiritual exercise, if I may say, to reengage with the systems that sustain us."[48] As well as mediating the private and the public, the table and pantry connect us to the global and cosmic order. The household becomes *oikos* in extremis.

Kingsolver's narrative and natural theology should be familiar to readers of her other works. Her celebrated novel *The Poisonwood Bible* (1998) recounts the story of Nathan Price, a Baptist preacher turned African missionary, who leads his family into the wilderness, where, he warns them, "there will *be* no buyers and sellers at all . . . not so much as a Piggly Wiggly." Although their mission is restricted to a year—"not enough time for going plumb crazy," as one daughter observes—disaster befalls the family, which suffers for Nathan's pride. His hubristic intention is signaled in the book's epigraph, from Genesis 1:28: "And God said unto them, Be fruitful, and multiply, and replenish the earth, and subdue it: and have dominion over the fish of the sea, and over the fowl of the air, and over every living thing that moveth upon the earth." But Africa will not be subdued.

The Price family's failure is foretold in food. They arrive in Africa packing four boxes of Betty Crocker cake mix—one for each girl's birthday—and a packet of seeds from their Texas kitchen garden, from which they plan to plant a "demonstration garden" that will "demonstrate to all of Africa how to grow crops." Despite the father's belief that "it's God's own will to cultivate the soil!" the crops fail, as do the cake mixes, and the family is forced to survive without the alimentary comforts of home.[49]

The failure of the family's domestic crops enacts in small the failed history of cultivation that underlies the Dutch conquest of central Africa and Africans in the slave trade. On their first arrival, daughter Leah recounts, European colonials "were dismayed to find no commodity agriculture," which foiled their hopes to conquer and develop the land: "All food was consumed very near to where it was grown. And so no cities, no giant plantations, and no roads necessary for transporting produce from the one to the other." In the absence of cash crops, the Dutch commodified the Africans themselves, a process that they initiated by converting them: "Soon the priests were holding mass baptisms on shore and marching their converts onto ships bound for sugar plantations in Brazil, slaves to the higher god of commodity agriculture."[50] Thus the book joins human and natural conquest with enforced religion: all are expressions of the misguided effort to subdue and extend dominion "over every living thing that moveth upon the earth."

Leah comes to seek a personal remedy to this brutal history of Western conquest in both agriculture and religion. "To be here without doing everything wrong requires a new agriculture, a new sort of planning, a new religion. I am the unmissionary," she declares near the end of the book, "beginning each day on my knees, asking to be converted." Where slavery had its origins in an agriculture and religion of conquest, Leah aspires to a new agriculture and religion of the home, one that honors the native practice of the Congo, whose people "merely lived in place and ate what they had."[51] Where the lack of commodity agriculture dismayed the Dutch, Leah learns to adapt to African ways of growing and consuming food in a place of no buyers and sellers. Learning to nourish her family and community from their own land, Leah professes, manifests a "trust in Creation" that forms the seed of a redeeming "new religion."

Kingsolver's Leah recalls the sensitive Leah of Genesis, a point accentuated by her contrast with her vain sister Rachel. To recall Dante, speaking in Leah's voice:

> my sister Rachel
> never deserts her mirror; there she sits
> all day; she longs to see her fair eyes gazing,
> as I, to see my hands adorning, long:
> she is content with seeing, I with labor.

The parallels between the novel's two sisters and their name-sakes are subtle but unmistakable. Like Dante's Rachel, King-solver's is beautiful and identified with a mirror—in this case, an "ivory plastic hand mirror with powdered-wig ladies on the back," one of the few possessions the family brings from home. At the end of the book, Kingsolver's Rachel runs a luxury hotel, by whose pool she enjoys lounging, though she admits sadness at the fact that, like her biblical namesake, "I never was able to have children."[52] Leah, by contrast, is a fruitful activist, making a home for her African husband and four sons.

If Rachel and Leah represent lives of leisure and work, con-templation and action, they also reflect, in Kingsolver's treat-ment, alternate approaches to Africa and the world. Rachel sur-vives by shutting out threat: "If there's ugly things going on out there, well, you put a good stout lock on your door and check it twice before you go to sleep. You focus on getting your own one little place set up perfect, as I have done, and you'll see. Other people's worries do not necessarily have to drag you down."[53] Leah, on the other hand, accepts that her home embraces and contains the world: "The equator just about runs smack-dab through our bed," which she calls "our nation of two." "In our bed, which Anatole calls the New Republic of Conubia, my husband tells me the history of the world."[54] For Kingsolver, the new religion belongs to the fertile, hardworking Leah, who, on behalf of a damaged world, embraces "the toils and hazards of the active life" that Augustine associated with her biblical forebear. Leah's domesticity represents not a shutting out of the world but an effort to embrace and heal it, and thereby to repair the ravages of global commodity markets that exploit and despoil both land and people.

If Leah's home contains, and potentially repairs, the world, so does Kingsolver's. As she asserts in *Animal, Vegetable, Miracle*, "becoming a less energy-dependent nation may just need to start with a good breakfast"[55] (5). Like a benign Nathan Price, Kingsolver leads her husband and daughters on yearlong sojourn in the wilderness, but contrary to Nathan's example, her family follows the example of the people of the Congo in *The Poisonwood Bible*, locavores for whom "all food was consumed very near to where it was grown." Where commodity agriculture is the root of colonial conquest in *Poisonwood Bible*, Kingsolver, like Leah, combats it by practicing domestic cultivation, thus rejecting global agribusiness, and its "commodity crops destined to become soda pop and cheap burgers."[56]

In Kingsolver's work, domesticity is reclaimed as the site of a new sacrality—one that repairs the depredations of the world by restoring the native holiness of Creation, the deity in Kingsolver's "new religion" in both *The Poisonwood Bible* and *Animal, Vegetable, Miracle*. In place of a merely personal search for the sacred, Kingsolver reimagines the sacred as a place that joins private and public, individual and global, active and contemplative. In a pointed revision of the traditions of reading the contemplative Rachel and the active Leah, Kingsolver's self-contemplating Rachel seeks a sanctuary from the world in her gated hotel. Meanwhile, the hard-working Leah makes her home a place where both world and work can be repaired and remade as sites of deep meaning, with global consequences. In keeping with our current identification with, and recuperation of, Martha as a spiritual figure and model, today's sacred domesticity brings together the worldly and the spiritual under one roof.

· 6 ·

A Life of Meaning
in a Market World

Now comes the time to grapple with some heroes, writers and artists who have helped us not only to understand the frantic and hyperactive condition of our lives but also to craft mental defenses against the sense of being the plaything of invisible forces. A perhaps unspoken theme of this book has been how uncomfortable an imbalance between action and contemplation can feel. The discomfort may be vague and hard to diagnose. These writers and artists are also moral clinicians and therapists, in the ancient sense. They show exactly where the sore spots are and may even help us purge the discomfort.

One of these heroes is Marian Evans, better known as George Eliot, the artist who perhaps most fully explored action's relation to contemplative states of the soul. Her novel *Middlemarch* (1874) is that most paradoxical of creatures, an epic of contemplation—a seemingly impossible form in which she achieves greatness. Eliot was able to express the condition of being a highly reflective creature thrown into a world of flux and asked to compose a meaningful life with whatever tools come to hand. Another hero is Herman Melville, creator of Bartleby the Scrivener, one of the most poignant anticapitalist martyrs in literary history.

An abiding question in theology has been How can I fashion a life in this world so that I can be saved in the next? The debate between the active life and the contemplative life offers a secular equivalent: How can I fashion a life of meaning in a world where our de facto religion is money and practical utility? Both Eliot and Melville are obsessed with this question in its secular, modern form. In their writings, the question is transformed into one of the deepest moral questions possible: How can we create an integrated self in a world that encourages us to treat people as means to an end not as ends in themselves?

George Eliot was remarkably prophetic about the rise of market and consumer society. She was a passionate and highly gifted writer, a woman whose fierce and searching intellect made her a far outlier among her contemporaries. *Middlemarch* is her masterpiece. The very title is ambiguous, evoking both the middle of a boundary and a march into the middle of things, a beginning in medias res, an epic beginning. How does a contemplative person live an epic or active life in the modern world when he or she is tossed, in a sense, into the middle of things? As critic Bernard Paris puts it, "The great question for Eliot, as well as for many of her contemporaries and ours, was, how can man lead a meaningful, morally satisfying life in an absurd universe."[1]

An absurd universe is a dangerous universe, and Eliot believed that young souls are particularly likely to be bruised and battered by their passage into the world: "Many souls in their young nudity are tumbled out among incongruities and left to 'find their feet' among them."[2] One of her favorite paintings was the *Sistine Madonna* by Raphael. In her journal, she records seeing it for the first time during a trip to Dresden:

I sat down on the sofa opposite the picture for an instant, but a sort of awe, as if I were suddenly in the living pres-

FIGURE 7. Raphael, *The Sistine Madonna*, ca. 1512/13. Oil on canvas, 269.5 × 301 cm. Gemäldegalerie Alte Meister, Dresden (inv. gal. nr. 93). Photography: Elke Estel/Hans-Peter Klut. Photograph: bpk, Berlin/Art Resource, New York.

ence of some glorious being, made my heart swell too much for me to remain comfortably, and we hurried out of the room.³

What moved her so much about Raphael's painting? Mary and her baby step down off a cloud and into our world. Pope Sixtus and Saint Barbara guide them. Mary and the baby are anxious. Mary looks down toward the path she will be walking. Her mouth is set and her eyes are tense. Her baby stares out at us in fear, shrinking back into his mother's neck. Does he know what we are going to do to him? He is a young soul about to be tumbled out, then set upon and tortured.

Marian Evans loved art. She was a passionately religious teenager, but she renounced her evangelical beliefs as a young woman. She came to see art—perhaps especially her chosen art, the novel—as a replacement for Christianity. She talked of writing as a struggle to "incarnate" ideas:

> I have gone through again and again the severe effort of trying to make certain ideas thoroughly incarnate, as if they had revealed themselves to me first in the flesh and not in the spirit. I think aesthetic teaching is the highest of all teaching because it deals with life in its highest complexity.

But, she adds, when aesthetic teaching "ceases to be purely aesthetic—if it lapses anywhere from the picture to the diagram—it becomes the most offensive of all teaching."⁴

Reform is Eliot's subject in small ways and large. She wrote *Middlemarch* in the 1870s, while Britain was debating the Second Reform Bill. She set it in the 1830s, at the time of the First Reform Bill. Both bills would extend the franchise and seek to remedy corrupt election practices. A reader could be forgiven for thinking her a pessimist about reform. She believes that in modern life, action is a tricky matter, almost impossible to get right. Her characters bear the brunt of her pessimism. Actions almost never work out as planned. The results are often ambiguous—can we even say that actions come to fruition in any recognizable way? Sometimes it is hard to tell. A character might pursue an action only to find it blocked by other people, or might see his actions carried through indirectly and long after the fact, as though some other force were needed to complete them. And sometimes characters' actions bring about results opposite to those they intended.

These are the situations that draw Eliot's deepest interest. A father faces the unpleasant task of saying no to his spoiled daughter and finds reason after reason to delay the unpleasant task:

> In the earlier half of the day there was business to hinder any formal communication of an adverse resolve; in the later there was dinner, wine, whist, and general satisfaction. And in the meanwhile the hours were each leaving their little deposit and gradually forming the final reason for inaction, namely, that action was too late.[5]

The hours leave their little deposits and soon, before anybody has ever really intended it, the moment for acting is over. Wordsworth famously "crossed the alps without knowing it," and Eliot is fascinated by how that can happen. Because she is a pessimist, for the most part, these deposits of inaction are tragic. Her hero Lydgate feels himself to be like Gulliver on Lilliput, tied down by invisible but unbreakable threads. In one subplot, he is the deciding vote on a contentious local political issue, an issue that pits his conscience against his desire to curry favor with his patron. And suddenly he is forced to choose: "For the first time Lydgate was feeling the hampering threadlike pressure of small social conditions, and their frustrating complexity."[6]

. . .

The character who most painfully bears the brunt of Eliot's interest in how action can go awry is the clergyman Edward Casaubon. For years Casaubon has been working on a book, *The Key to All Mythologies*, a massive synthesis of world mythology. (For a scholar to read about him is to wince in painful recognition.) Casaubon has gathered reams of materials but has trouble actually writing anything. He compiles ever more research, collating and cross-indexing what he finds. Eliot profoundly identified with his plight. She wrote in a letter to Harriet Beecher Stowe that "the Casaubon-tints are not quite foreign to my own mental complexion."[7] Yet she criticizes him sharply. He fails as an author, she thinks, because he refuses to examine what really drives him. His one bit of actual writing—a codicil to his will in which he forbids his young wife Dorothea from marrying his handsome young cousin in the event of his death—brings about the very result he intended to prevent. In short, actions go awry when they are uncoupled from the inner life.

Other characters suffer the effects of her interest in different ways. She is fascinated by the figure of the idealistic young person who gets pushed (like the infant in Raphael's painting) out of his or her chosen path and into another one. We may think of our lives as an arc, with a beginning, middle, and end, but that sense of an arc is an illusion. Indeed, our lives are much more like webs, branching out in infinite directions. The character who embodies this idea for Eliot is Saint Teresa of Avila, a sixteenth-century Spanish mystic who was famous for her religious visions and for her vows of poverty and renunciation. Teresa saw the Catholic church as spiritually lax and too interested in worldly power and money, so she founded a religious order that would be poor and spiritually pure, and dedicated herself to contemplative prayer. But that was in the sixteenth century. In the modern world, such reforms no longer seem possible. "Many Theresas have been born who found for themselves no epic life wherein there was a constant unfolding of far-resonant action," Eliot writes in the novel's prelude. Not only are we tumbled out into an absurd world, but providence offers no help in guiding our actions. The novel's heroine makes a giant mistake with her very first step into adulthood. She marries a man whom everybody around her can see is a disastrous choice, and she does so out of the most idealistic motives, thinking naively that "it would be like marrying Pascal." With no Providence to guide us, our paths through life can seem purposeless. "With dim lights and tangled circumstance" these failed Theresas have "tried to shape their thought and deed in noble agreement." The plight of the modern reformer is to have her efforts "dispersed among hindrances, instead of centring in some long-recognizable deed." That plight is made worse by the fact that action and contemplation ("thought and deed") have come so far apart.

Eliot saw that a person can start out headed in one direction in life and end up in a completely unanticipated place. Her tragic hero, the young doctor Tertius Lydgate, moves to the town of Middlemarch with high hopes of reforming the medical profession and inventing a new method for treating fevers. He ends up as a gout doctor in a spa town—roughly the equivalent of a plastic surgeon in a wealthy suburb. How does this happen? What prevents people from achieving their goals? What mix of character and circumstance gets in people's way?

Lydgate's life is ruined by marrying a woman selfish to her very core. His own flawed personality lies at the root of his disastrous choice. He has, in Eliot's devastating phrase, "spots of commonness"—a group of prejudices that "in spite of noble intentions and sympathy, were half of them such as are found in ordinary men of the world: that distinction of mind which belonged to his intellectual ardor, did not penetrate his feeling and judgment about furniture, or women, or the desirability of its being known (without his telling) that he was better born than other country surgeons."[8] He applies his brilliant mind to science but not more pedestrian affairs—nor indeed does he examine his own tacit feeling of social superiority. And so he marries someone who expresses all the desire for social status that he cannot. The unhappy marriage sucks the marrow out of his life. He dies young, bitterly joking that his wife had murdered his soul.

Forces much larger and more impersonal than our own private failings can also knock us off our chosen paths. College students today often speak sincerely of wanting to have an "impact" on the world. But having an impact (or as Eliot put it, having one's efforts "center in some long-recognizable deed") is a noble but ultimately quixotic wish. Eliot specializes in all the ways such a wish can be thwarted or can change over time, imperceptibly, to a different wish. But such a wish also butts up against the nature of actions themselves. To destroy is much easier than to build. Destroying can be done in seconds; building takes slow, infinite patience. Our so-called impact is just as likely to be negative or neutral as it is to be positive. But of course, nobody wants to think of one's own impact like that. Nor do many students really imagine that the outcome of their far-resonant actions will be unknown. Yet the nature of the ever-branching web is such that our actions are refracted into a million dispersed lights. If Eliot foresaw all of this, she could hardly have foreseen how enormous, how all-encompassing the web would grow. World economies and cultures are now so closely knit that even tiny actions spread further, with less-knowable outcomes, than ever before.

Here is a rather fanciful example of a latter-day Theresa such as Eliot had in mind. The example is drawn from the life (still in glorious progress) of somebody who by any measure began her life as a reformer and has had epic adventures, setbacks, and triumphs, and more setbacks. In late May of 1969, Hillary D. Rodham, the student body president at Wellesley College, gave a commencement speech to her graduating class. She was twenty-one years old. In the audience was Senator Edward Brooke of Massachusetts, the first African American elected to the US Senate. That spring had been filled with mass protests against the Vietnam War. Rodham's speech feels politically urgent; she even begins by criticizing Senator Brooke for calling for empathy. Empathy doesn't go far enough, she says. Nor do statistics about poverty. We need not "social reconstruction" but "human reconstruction." "The struggle for an integrated life existing in an atmosphere of communal trust and respect is one with desperately important political and social consequences," she says. The challenge for members of her class is nothing less than integrating themselves as they reform a broken, messy, too-complicated world:

> We are, all of us, exploring a world that none of us even understands and attempting to create within that uncertainty. But there are some things we feel, feelings that our prevailing, acquisitive, and competitive corporate life, including tragically the universities, is not the way of life for us. We're searching for more immediate, ecstatic and

penetrating mode of living. And so our questions, our questions about our institutions, about our colleges, about our churches, about our government continue. . . . One of the most tragic things that happened yesterday, a beautiful day, was that I was talking to a woman who said that she wouldn't want to be me for anything in the world. She wouldn't want to live today and look ahead to what it is she sees because she's afraid. Fear is always with us but we just don't have time for it. Not now.[9]

Of course her views have changed. But sometimes it is striking to see the change in action. In late April 2008, Hillary Rodham Clinton, now a senator herself, was running for president of the United States for the first time. Locked in a fierce battle for the Democratic nomination, she was pressuring her Senate colleague Barack Obama from the right. As the endless contest juddered into Indiana, Senator Clinton sat down for an interview with Bill O'Reilly, the proudly contrarian, blustering, right-wing political talk show host. (O'Reilly, Rush Limbaugh, Sean Hannity, and others had been meddling in Democratic Party primaries, stumping for Hillary on the presumption that she would be easier to beat in the general election.) O'Reilly came out swinging. He bristled with fake outrage about Obama's statements, associates, and positions, daring Senator Clinton to agree with him. Then came this exchange:

CLINTON: No, I'm not waffling. I'm saying I'm not going to impose additional burdens on middle-class families. And there are a lot of people . . .
O'REILLY: But I'm not a middle-class family. I'm a rich guy.
CLINTON: Well, and you know what? Rich people, God bless us. We deserve all the opportunities . . .

O'REILLY: All right.

CLINTON: . . . to make sure our country and our blessings continue to the next generation.

To some extent this example is unfair. Hillary Clinton was a successful politician in 1968 when she praised transcendence over acquisitiveness, and she was a successful politician in 2008 when she preached the gospel of wealth and a low estate-tax rate. Successful politicians have to tell people what they want to hear. She told her Wellesley graduating class that they were going to find more ecstatic modes of living. She told Bill O'Reilly that rich people should be given the opportunity to pass their wealth unhindered down to future generations. She seeks to be all things to all people. The example is unfair because it is being told as a story—a story with a somewhat moralizing point. And maybe the real moral is this: only very lucky people get to live out this sort of story—people who live passionately enough and long enough to find their commitments changing, and who are lucky enough to have other people paying close attention to what they say. Movement like this proves nothing more than that a person is alive and growing. And it is precisely this sort of (apparent) reversal that interests George Eliot: stories have lives of own that we cannot predict or foresee, much less control.

Hilary Clinton, the politician and very public face, the idealistic young reformer turned establishment icon, may also (loosely) illustrate another abiding concern of Eliot's, namely her deep and insightful critique of the pressures capitalism puts on people, especially when we allow our deepest selves to be made into marketable commodities. In another of *Middlemarch*'s concurrent plots, Eliot tells the story of the town banker, Nicholas Bulstrode. As a lowly young banker's clerk, Bulstrode joined a dissenting congregation in a London suburb. He was incredibly happy. Looking back on that period, he deems it "the spot he would have chosen now to awake in and find the rest a dream." Then something happens. He becomes friendly with the richest man in the congregation, Mr. Dunkirk. An orphan who had been educated at a state charity school, Bulstrode is awed and touched by Dunkirk's attentions. But he also begins to have grander ambitions—to imagine the "prospects of 'instrumentality' towards the uniting of distinguished religious gifts with successful business." So he starts visiting Dunkirk's house, and eventually, when a partner in Dunkirk's firm dies, is hired into the job. Soon Bulstrode realizes that Dunkirk, a pawnbroker, has a profitable sideline in fencing stolen goods. At first he finds this distasteful, but then he starts to justify it to himself. Even if he profits from human misery, he thinks, he can use those profits in the service of godly ends. Speaking to God, he says, "Thou knowest how loose my soul sits from these things—how I view them all as implements for tilling Thy garden rescued here and there from the wilderness." He spreads soothing balm on his conscience. But then trouble comes. Dunkirk's daughter had run away when she discovered what the business was all about. At first, the Dunkirk family didn't mind too much because they also had a son, and as Eliot's memorable line has it, "the daughter was at a discount." But soon the son dies, and then Dunkirk dies too. Bulstrode wants to marry Dunkirk's widow, but she has "qualms and yearnings about her daughter"—or, to be more precise, having lost her son, she hopes that maybe her daughter has had a son of her own, so she can have a grandson. She asks Bulstrode to help locate her daughter. He tells her he has tried but can find no information. In fact, the man he hired, the disreputable John Raffles, has found the daughter, but Bulstrode pays him to keep that information to himself.

Now, many years later, Mrs. Dunkirk too has died, and Bulstrode is happily remarried. He has grown very wealthy. But he is also anxious, pompous, controlling, and meddlesome, using his money to control people and to play politics. An elder in his church, he has made a bargain with God: to atone for his sins, he will allow God to use him as an "instrument" of his will. So who should turn up but Raffles, now in the later stages of alcoholic disease and demanding more hush money. Bulstrode promptly pays him a hundred pounds, and Raffles goes away for a while. But soon he's back, and Bulstrode figures that he should tell Will Ladislaw the whole story. He summons Ladislaw and tells him that he has no legal claim on Bulstrode, but he does have a moral one. He offers Will five hundred pounds a year and, upon Bulstrode's death, a chunk of capital. Will refuses the money and tells Bulstrode that his grandfather's business was dishonorable and that he would give all of his own money to anybody who could disprove the story of his disreputable connections. Finally Raffles dies in Bulstrode's house, and everybody assumes that Bulstrode murdered him. Bulstrode is forced to leave Middlemarch in disgrace.

The Raffles plot—sensational and melodramatic—can seem like an alien life form grafted into the novel, but Eliot uses the theme of blackmail to make a broader point. She is deeply interested in whether we are threatened by the rise of an all-knowing information culture—a culture in which everyone knows everyone else's business.[10] (To watch her grapple with this question, a century before the rise of mass-market celebrity culture, is stunning.) What does it mean to be a public figure in an age in which anyone can rustle through your trash—figuratively speaking—and find out your deepest, darkest secrets? Marian Evans was actually quite worried about being blackmailed. Not only was she living with a man who was legally married to another woman, but she did not want to be exposed as the person behind the George Eliot pen name.[11] She valued privacy—and indeed, secrecy. In a culture that doesn't value either, she thought, blackmail is the new fate, the finger of an all-knowing providence that will expose you.

But her worries about blackmail go even deeper. Blackmail is a classic legal and economic puzzle. The puzzle is, why should it be illegal? Here is a thought experiment. Suppose you go to a party, and there you meet a gorgeous and mysterious stranger. The stranger looks at you with deep brown liquid eyes, presses a cold beverage into your hands, and soon you find yourself. . . . We'll skip over this bit, but let's just say that you have a really nice time hanging out. Alas, in the sober light of morning, you find yourself regretting some decisions that were made the evening before (note your judicious use of the passive voice). You regret these things because, in fact, you have a devoted partner whom you love very much and plan on marrying someday, a partner who happens to be out of town visiting an aging grandmother in a nursing home and helping a younger brother through a personal crisis. A partner who is a saint—a lovely, perfect, kind, decent saint who would take an exceedingly dim view of any lightsome frolic—however innocent—with a stranger at a party, and who will almost certainly drop you like a brick if you are found out.

Now it happens that you have a nominal friend who has been paying close attention to your doings. She knows what you got up to at that party. Your friend is a stern and unforgiving moralist, rigid and inflexible in her views of right and wrong. She points the finger of righteousness at you and calls you to account. She will expose you as a love rat. Your friend doesn't want to hear that the flesh is weak and the drinks were cold. She believes that every right-thinking person in the universe would roundly condemn your actions.

But wait. There is one more thing. Your saintly partner also happens to be the scion of a major American industrial fortune, and you, being a bit on the lazy side, have been looking forward to a life spent jetting around the world, sitting by pools, being waited on by a bevy of discreet servants. What if your friend were suddenly to discover some patches of flexibility in her moralism? Rather than calling you out as a rat, she sees a way to supplement her somewhat meager income and comes to you with a straightforward business deal: pay her some small percentage of your future income, and she won't spill the beans. You have a strong incentive to pay up. If you can just get your partner to the altar, you'll have more money than you can possibly spend in a lifetime. So why not funnel a bit of it in her direction? It seems like a win-win situation. What could possibly be better?

It's blackmail. But why should that be a problem? Why should the law care about the side deal you and your friend plan to make? In meeting a stranger at a party, you haven't broken any laws, so you aren't paying her to cover up a crime. Is your agreement that much different from any other contract you could make? Maybe the problem is that you can't opt out. But any contract has some coerciveness built in. Your friend would also love to lounge around with jet-setters, but instead she sets her alarm for 4:30, wakes up with a jolt, fumbles for her glasses, makes a cup of coffee, grabs her keys, and heads out the door to the bus stop. She stands in the cold and dark and waits for her bus, all so she can finish some crucial paperwork before the office opens. It's true that nobody coerced her into doing any of that, but there is an implied threat, one that she internalized long ago. Suppose she just turned off the alarm, went back to sleep, missed her bus, skipped work, and had a fun day shopping, eating a leisurely lunch with a few glasses of wine, then curling up in front of an old movie. However lovely that might be in the short run, in the long run it would be bad—with consequences for her reputation, her continued employment, and any interests dependent on her income. So how do we explain why blackmail—a simple contract where you pay your friend to keep your secret—should be illegal but having a job—a contract where your friend exchanges her labor for money—is not only legal but an expected part of life? Each seems to be a simple matter of incentives. Your friend offers you incentives to pay money to cover up your moral turpitude. Her boss offers similarly strong incentives to get her to show up to work. Why should she be able to sell her labor but not her ability to keep a secret?

Now you could say you didn't enter into this contract freely, but your friend would retort that her job contract is not something that she freely entered into either. Her last name isn't Buffett, Gates, or Zuckerberg, and thus she is not exactly free to choose whether and where to work. And when you think about it, blackmail may not be all bad. After all, if you knew that someone was going to find out your secrets and demand money for keeping them, you might behave better in the first place. Why shouldn't we think of blackmail as an extra incentive program to reward good character? If blackmail were totally legal, not only would people shape up, but the blackmail contract would potentially be more stable. One big downside of giving in to your blackmailer is that she can come back at any point and unilaterally rewrite the terms of the contract. That's what happens to Eliot's banker when his drunken former employee reappears after a stint in America and demands more money. If blackmail were legal, maybe we could enforce the contract, holding the blackmailer to the original terms.

"One of the main reasons that blackmail is illegal (and strongly perceived to be wrong)," writes legal theorist James Boyle, "is that there is a strong social belief, sometimes consciously articulated and sometimes unconsciously held, that not everything should be reduced to the 'universalizing logic of the money relation.' In particular, the private realm of home and hearth should be protected against the relentless instrumentalism of market transactions."[12] After Marian Evans was revealed to be behind the Eliot pen name, she wrote "I only wish I could write something that would contribute to heighten men's reverence before the secrets of each other's souls, that there might be less assumption of entire knowingness, as a datum from which inferences are to be drawn."[13] George Eliot was smart and financially successful. She benefited from market society. But she worried about the effect of markets on personhood, about what happens when you lose your sense of privacy. When personal information becomes a commodity, she suggests, then a drunken ex-employee turned blackmailer can become the new face of Fate.

Middlemarch argues, insofar as novels make arguments, that market economies give people strong incentives to treat each other as things, not people. The town banker puts his conscience up for sale, allowing himself to be an "instrument" or "implement" in God's hands in payment for having made his fortune by stealing and lying. He dons the breastplate of righteousness. But when it turns out that a disgruntled former employee is running the show rather than God, his bargain begins to look like a very bad gamble indeed. The banker has woven his worldly and spiritual ambitions together in a way that turns out to be fatal to both. But is there any other choice? Do any of us fare better in marrying the worldly and the spiritual, the active and contemplative sides of our natures? Let us turn now to a writer who diagnosed the very same tensions and gave us an enduring mythology for resolving them.

Bartleby the Scrivener, Herman Melville's 1853 tale of Wall Street, shows us how Bulstrode might have acted had he decided to hold on to his integrity. Bartleby works as a copyist in a law office. His boss is a lazy sort of fellow who believes that "the easiest way is best." The boss rates people on how "useful" they are to him. At first a model employee, Bartleby soon stops doing his work. Asked to copy documents, Bartleby says that he would "prefer not to." His boss tries to reason with him, to no avail. The boss then tries to find him another job, but Bartleby would prefer not to do any other work. He won't say why not. In fact, he withdraws from social commerce altogether. Bartleby dies in the Tombs, a New York jail, after refusing to eat.

Bartleby the Scrivener has been widely seen as Melville's blast against the publishing industry. Having been wildly successful in his twenties publishing tales about his adventures in the South Seas, he tried writing more experimental fiction. His efforts failed badly. *Moby Dick* was a publishing disaster. Melville was acutely distressed, as revealed in a letter to his best friend Nathaniel Hawthorne: "What I feel most moved to write, that is banned, it will not pay. Yet, altogether, write the other way I cannot. So the product is a final hash and all my books are botches." Bartleby stops cooperating when his boss simply hands him a paper without looking up at him:

> In my haste and natural expectancy of instant compliance, I sat with my head bent over the original on my desk, and my right hand sideways, and somewhat nervously extended with the copy, so that immediately upon emerging from his retreat, Bartleby might snatch it and proceed to business without the least delay. In this very attitude did I sit when I called to him, rapidly stating what it was I wanted him to do—namely, to examine a small paper with me. Imagine my surprise, nay, my consternation, when without moving from his privacy, Bartleby in a singularly mild, firm voice, replied, "I would prefer not to."

The boss uses Bartleby as a tool. He does not see the human being standing in front of him. Bartleby seems to decide that if being treated this way is what the marketplace offers him, he will not engage. Melville, too, withdrew from writing. He went to work at the customs house in New York, developing a reputation as one of the only honest customs officers in a corrupt business. When he died, he was all but forgotten.

Bartleby embodies the negation of society even more potently than the American transcendentalists. Thoreau wrote, "Wherever a man goes, men will pursue and paw him with their dirty institutions, and, if they can, constrain him to belong to their desperate odd-fellow society." Surely, though, starving yourself to death in jail is an extreme way of stopping those dirty institutions from pawing you. Even Thoreau, thrown in jail for not paying his taxes, got sprung after one night. "It is true," he writes a bit ruefully, "I might have resisted forcibly with more or less effect, might have run 'amok' against society; but I preferred that society should run 'amok' against me, it being the desperate party." How far does a person need to go to keep his soul from being turned into a commodity? Which office clerk—Nicholas Bulstrode the bargainer, or Bartleby the naysayer, the outcast, the loner—has the better solution?

The answer, of course, is neither. Art can ask how to compose a self in a capitalist system in which souls seem to be for sale, but arguably art cannot answer that question, at least not in any final way. But that is the point. Melville and Eliot, writers born in the same year who died one year apart in very different states of fame, channel their impulses into a mode of expression that goes far beyond mere paraphrase.

And just occasionally they find a shining source of grace. Towards the end of *Middlemarch*, the heroine Dorothea Brooke suffers an emotional shock. Wanting to comfort a townswoman whose marriage is in crisis, Dorothea finds the woman deep in conversation with a man who is not her husband. As she comes upon the scene, two things strike her: first, that the man and woman must be lovers; second, that she herself loves the man (this sudden thought surprises and troubles her). During a long night spent sobbing out her grief, Dorothea has an epiphany. She sees the other woman, the man, and herself as fellow creatures caught in a web, each bearing the crushing burden of solitary consciousness. Dorothea wants to offer compassion rather than recoiling in scorn or spite. But the question of how to act presses up inside her:

> She yearned towards the perfect Right, that it might make a throne within her, and rule her errant will. "What should I do—how should I act now, this very day if I could clutch my own pain, and compel it to silence, and think of those three!"

While Dorothea's anguished query—"how should I act"?—flares up out of a local trouble, her cry speaks to the novel's ultimate concern. Indeed, since Eliot's subject is the growth of the modern world, Dorothea's question echoes out of the soul of each of her more self-aware characters. To wonder how to act is to face a plight forced on us by the gifts of leisure and the unchecked profusion of choices. To be modern is to be free to choose our home, profession, mate, and—most dramatically—our own values. Yet to be free to choose these things also puts great strain on us. How is any of us supposed to know what to choose or how? What do we do when we find ourselves having to compose our own life, our own soul?

Eliot could hardly have foreseen how freedom of choice would become the greatest human good of the consumer age, at least by the lights of the free market. But she had a hunch that too much free choice could make people anxious, alienated, stressed, and worried. Her hunch has been amply confirmed by research into "choice overload." Psychologists have found that having too many choices makes us anxious and jittery. As the number of options goes up, we become less likely to choose anything at all—whether in simple matters like flavors of jam or chocolate or weightier matters like whether to write an extra-credit essay in a class.[14] Faced with more choices, we become paralyzed. Why? When we choose one thing, we forgo another—and then wonder whether we did the right thing. Doubt, regret, self-criticism, and remorse are effects of having to leave behind all the things we didn't choose. As the number of choices we have to make every day gets bigger, so too do our feelings of regret and self-doubt.

Some writers argue that people should develop simple rules for making choices and stick to them.[15] If you always order a grande skim no-foam latte in the morning, you don't have to worry about the ever-greater number of ways to mix your coffee and milk. But simple rules work don't work well when product innovations move so quickly that any set-it-and-forget-it style choice seems bound to be pathetically outdated in a few seconds. And the choice of morning coffee is only one of hundreds of minor choices we are asked to make every day. Every store, website, and restaurant—not to mention phone plan, health plan, retirement plan, and insurance salesman—dazzles us with an array of choices.[16] The unstated assumption of this economic environment is that having more choices is better. But "as the number of options under consideration goes up and the attractive features associated with the rejected alternatives accumulate, the satisfaction derived from the chosen alternative will go down."[17] In addition, one cruel fact about happiness is that we adapt to it, so the pleasure we get from a satisfying choice doesn't tend to last.

George Eliot was not thinking about consumer psychology.

But she was unusually perceptive about human feeling. She knew what it was be a sensitive intelligent being thrown into the jostling world and asked to fashion a self out of whatever materials come to hand. And so she painted a scene to make vivid her heroine's plight. As the morning dawns, Dorothea quiets her anguish and has a new vision:

> It had taken long for her to come to that question, and there was light piercing into the room. She opened her curtains, and looked out towards the bit of road that lay in view, with fields beyond, outside the entrance-gates. On the road there was a man with a bundle on his back and a woman carrying her baby; in the field she could see figures moving—perhaps the shepherd with his dog. Far off in the bending sky was the pearly light; and she felt the largeness of the world and the manifold wakings of men to labour and endurance. She was a part of that involuntary, palpitating life, and could neither look out on it from her luxurious shelter as a mere spectator, nor hide her eyes in selfish complaining.
>
> What she would resolve to do that day did not yet seem quite clear, but something that she could achieve stirred her as with an approaching murmur which would soon gather distinctness.[18]

The light piercing into the room represents enlightenment. But what sort of enlightenment is this? The heroine opens her curtains and outside she sees a small bit of the road, but her view expands until everything merges together and she feels herself fused with the active world in ways that have no rational plot. Still unanswered are the questions of what to do, how to act. The answer may come, but not through reason.

An astute literary critic, D. A. Miller, locates the sources of the heroine's unease in her being a member of the leisure class: "To the figures in the landscape, of course, physical labor and child-bearing have an immediate and unquestioned relevance. Dorothea's situation, however, is precisely one in which work and womanhood have become problems."[19] It is tempting to imagine that other beings—beings different from us by gender, race, class, or even species—have some closer, more necessary, and therefore less troubled relationship to action than we do. To be human, it seems, is to imagine both a paradise that is elsewhere, ever receding into the distance, and some other beings who are standing there enjoying it. Those other beings seem magically unimpeded by angst, neurotic self-reflection, or anomie. They appear to inhabit a wondrous plenitude where tools spring easily to hand, where causes and effects are closely knit, and where the seeds of action bear early and faithful fruit.

Over the past century and a half, a newer reverie has grown, clinging like ivy to this older one. Capitalism and consumerism leave us in a state of recurring psychic distress because our wants can only be briefly and sporadically met. Consumerism implants desires for an ever-swelling range of goods. We want them, we buy them, the thrill wears off, and then we want new or different things. Our wanting becomes chronic, leaving us materially rich but spiritually shivering and skeletal. Meanwhile a fantasy grows inside our disrupted selves that unity is elsewhere. Perhaps laborers or rustics or indigenous peoples or yogis mesh with their habitats more smoothly than the restless, neurotic moneyed burghers of the rootless present.

Is this the fantasy gripping Eliot's heroine as she looks out the window at the man with his bundle and the woman with her baby? Certainly Dorothea has the leisure and income not to worry about labor and childbearing, and the time to spend worrying about how to live. But is it a problem of the middle class? Or of the nature of a sensitive intellectual being? Or of a being who finds herself inside a story whose beginning and ending are murky at best?

Eliot never tells us which of these choices is hers. She warned us, after all, that fiction with a message would not be fiction. She conspicuously refuses to give a conventional ending to her novel. Indeed, the novel's narrator withdraws markedly from the characters. The narrator retreats, standing in an ambivalent and divided posture toward the people she has been telling about for so many pages. She stands in the same relationship to her characters as the heroine stands to those distant laboring figures in the landscape—in other words, she contemplates them from a distance. Both are "part of that involuntary, palpitating life" they see before them. Both are poised on the border, the windowsill between themselves and the characters they look at. To write a contemplative novel—an epic of contemplation—is to live on the boundary between yourself and other people, between watching and doing. The pain and glory of being such creatures as we are is to feel that tension and to resist the sometimes overwhelming impulse to close it down.

· · ·

Why not try to end with some good news? Or on a more optimistic note? After all, the frenzy of our current plight will change. Writers like George Eliot and Herman Melville are almost scarily prophetic about the dystopian elements of consumer culture. But surely we can find other writers who offer us a happier vision, one that doesn't end in "I would prefer not to."

Let's turn to Franz Kafka. In 1913 Kafka was working at an office job at the Workers Accident Insurance Institute in his native city of Prague. He struggled desperately to find time to write stories. His effort was enormous, and so was the toll on his psyche. He worked in the office from early morning until mid-afternoon. Then he napped, did "ten minutes of exercises," and had dinner with his younger sisters. Finally,

> at 10:30 (but often not till 11:00) I sit down to write, and I go on, depending on my strength, inclination, and luck, until one, two, or three o'clock, once even till six in the morning. Then again exercises . . . a wash, and then usually with a slight pain in my heart and twitching stomach muscles, to bed. Then every imaginable effort to go to sleep . . . thus the night consists of two parts: one wakeful, the other sleepless. . . . So it is hardly surprising if at the office the next morning, I only just manage to start work with what little strength is left.

His diary entries grew increasingly forlorn—"Angst, neurasthenia etc."—until suddenly he wrote several stories in three months, including "The Metamorphosis." He wrote this entry in his diary:

> The tremendous world I have inside my head, but how to free myself and free it without being torn to pieces. And a thousand times rather be torn to pieces than retain it in me or bury it. That, indeed, is why I am here, that is quite clear to me.[20]

Writers often refer to the tremendous worlds inside their heads, worlds that are sometimes more vivid, colorful, and present to them than the world outside. The eighteenth-century philosopher John Locke revealed his relationship to these two worlds in remarking, "however, I may be mistaken in what passes without me, I am infallible in what passes in my own mind."[21]

Writers have called this inner world a garden, a tract to till and cultivate. They have called it an ocean. Kafka called it a frozen sea ("ein Buch muß die Axt sein für das gefrorene Meer in uns. Das glaube ich"—A book must be an axe for the frozen sea inside us. I believe that). They have called it heaven and also hell. Milton's Satan muses, "The mind is its own place and can make a hell of heaven, a heaven of hell." The idea that the mind is a vast and separate space that we can fruitfully explore is central to art, central to literature, central to psychoanalysis, and now central to the convergence of neuroscience and mindfulness practice. The term "mindsight" comes from an emerging field in neuroscience. Daniel J. Siegel, a neuroscientist and psychiatrist, has written several books about the topic. Like Thoreau and many others, he argues that mindsight—the capacity to become consciously aware of our own inner landscape—is a practice that can be cultivated. Mindsight, he writes, is "the basic skill that underlies everything we mean when we speak of having social and emotional intelligence."[22]

Long before neuroscientists developed this approach, writers were passionate advocates for mindsight. Thoreau obsessively observed his inner landscape. "The poet," he wrote, "must be continually watching the moods of his mind, as the astronomer watches the aspects of the heavens." Rather than traveling to catalogue the natural world, he scolds us, we would do well to stay home and study the universe inside. And this practice is deeply, almost existentially, democratic. Thoughts are thoughts. They are equally powerful, equally worthy of study, no matter whose mind they happen to light upon. "A meteorological journal of the mind. You shall observe what occurs in your latitude, I in mine."[23]

Thoreau's friend and mentor Ralph Waldo Emerson made a lifetime study out of the "discrepance" between his inner landscape and the outer one. He tells us repeatedly how wide the gap between them is:

> I know that the world I converse with in the city and in the farms, is not the world I think. I observe that difference and shall observe it. One day, I shall know the value and law of this discrepance.

Like Plato and Kant and other idealist philosophers, Emerson believed that our real life lies beyond experience. Only the inner world touches on this real life, which Emerson thought came from the mind of God. The outer world is tricky and slippery. Or, as he put it somewhat obliquely, musing on the transience of the things he loved most, "I take this evanescence and lubricity of all objects, which lets them slip through our fingers then when we clutch hardest, to be the most unhandsome part of our condition." Objects appear stable, yet when we clutch at them, they slip out of our grasp and fade from view. So the only way to navigate is to trust our inner compass.

Emerson and Thoreau's literary precursors, the English Romantic poets, were arguably the first group of artists to grapple seriously with the "discrepance." A European movement that began in Germany in the late eighteenth century and eventually spread all over the world, Romanticism is still powerfully with us today. In the intensity of our creative ferment, in our confessional culture, in our belief that, as William Blake put it, we "must invent our own system or be enslaved by another man's," we are all post-Romantic. Indeed the most radical parts of Romanticism have now become accepted wisdom. We rarely doubt that the soul meshes badly with the material world. Poet after Romantic poet, painter after painter, gives voice not just to the rend in the fabric between inner and outer worlds, but to the pain that division creates. The poet in Shelley's "Alastor," for example, meets a swan. The swan can swim home to his mate, says the poet, but the poet remains stranded on the shore without a home, in one of the great images of the alienation between the inner and outer worlds:

> And what am I that I should linger here,
> With voice far sweeter than thy dying notes,
> Spirit more vast than thine, frame more attuned
> To beauty, wasting these surpassing powers
> In the deaf air, to the blind earth, and heaven
> That echoes not my thoughts?

In the preface to *Lyrical Ballads*, a revolutionary collection of poems that he wrote with Samuel Taylor Coleridge, William Wordsworth described the poet as having special powers of connection to his own mind. A poet, with his "disposition to be affected more than other men by absent things as if they were present," moves about in worlds not realized. For Wordsworth the mind is a conjurer whose magic is to bring the inner and outer worlds into contact with each other. The poet's mind exercises itself on its own passions to strengthen them, thereby creating passions that "more nearly resemble" those "produced by real events" than people with less developed mental powers are able to experience. But Wordsworth goes further. He makes strong claims about what you must do to become an artist. Not only do you need to accept that your soul is alienated, you need to be a brilliant psychologist, a fearless explorer of your inner world. And you cannot balk if you find that inner world populated by ugly misfits, by antisocial, angry, sexually monstrous characters. Wordsworth shows us all of these parts of himself, not proudly but painfully. He is not boasting, but neither is he projecting a false self.

Wordsworth, Kafka, Emerson, Thoreau, and many other artists have told us that their true story is the story of their inner lives. Readers long used to hearing such talk may dismiss it as so much myth-making or poetic fancy. But science is starting to tell its own story about the experience. Psychologists now recognize a long continuum between mechanistic ways of thinking (seeing the world as largely composed of bodies) and mentalistic ones (seeing it as largely composed of minds). Most of us balance these two ways of thinking, but tending toward either end can open fascinating wellsprings of creativity. People whose minds incline toward autistic spectrum disorders tend to systematize and mechanize, while those whose minds tend more toward psychotic spectrum disorders may discern shapes in the clouds, murmurs in the rustling of leaves, voices on the wind.[24] The sheer number of accounts of such experiences suggests that writers fall closer to the mentalizing than the mechanizing end of the spectrum. George Eliot, for example, recounts, "When I was quite a little child I could not be satisfied with the things around me; I was constantly living in a world of my own creation, and I was quite contented to have no companions that I might be left to my own musings and imagine scenes in which I was the chief actress. Conceive what a character novels would give to these Utopias. I was early supplied with them by those who kindly sought to gratify my appetite for reading, and of course I made use of the materials they supplied for building my castles in the air."[25]

Deep in writers' bones lurks the belief that, in order to flourish, action needs to put down roots in the inner life. The inner lives of writers may be as crowded, colorful, messy, and vital as a street fair on a sunny afternoon, but many writers argue that the key to acting well and effectively lies here, inside the carnival. Effective action is like an engine. The inner world is the crankshaft. If the pistons aren't attached, the cylinders cannot fire. If we do not have access to our interiority, some writers tell us, we will not have the capacity to act. Unless we take a good long look around inside, artists tell us over and over again, our actions will be deformed. Sometimes writers assert this belief merely by arching an eyebrow at someone whose actions have gone off the rails. After her husband died, Joan Didion came across a booklet from his Princeton class called "Lives of '54." One entry "was from Donald H. ('Rummy') Rumsfeld, who noted: 'After Princeton, the years seem like a blur, but the days seem more like rapid fire.' I thought about this."[26] *I thought about this*: the writer's response to the man of action. The moralist's response to the wayward warrior. Think, or your aim will be off.

Consider how artists portray athletes. The man or woman of action poses a unique challenge to the view that action and inwardness require each other. Athletes seem to embody what many writers say they crave: action uninfected by the roving, restless, neurotic, distracted mind. Don't think, do! But if athletes don't think, how can they do? David Foster Wallace wonders as much about Tracy Austin:

> How can great athletes shut off the Iago-like voice of the self? How can they bypass the head and simply and superbly act? How, at the critical moment, can they invoke for themselves a cliche as trite as "One ball at a time" or "Gotta concentrate here," and mean it, and then do it?[27]

How indeed can they do that? Brain scans of professional athletes show that the level of neural activation when competing is much lower than in the brains of novices.[28] The findings suggest that repeated practice makes movements so automatic that non-essential neural activity "selectively shuts down." More specifically, professional athletes temporarily shut down the memory-forming regions of the brain so as to maximize activity in centers that guide movement, which may explain why post-match commentary from athletes themselves yields comedy gold (e.g., the "Literary Football" sketch from *Monty Python's Flying Circus*[29]). "That's why they usually thank God or their moms," says cognitive psychologist Sian Beilock of the University of Chicago. "They don't know what they did, so they don't know what else to say."[30]

And yet, faced with such maddening quietude, writers often want to pry open athletes' minds and look inside. So David Foster Wallace responded when Tracy Austin published a tennis memoir. Both had been junior tennis players at the same time but playing at very different levels. Austin won a professional tournament at the age of fourteen and shot to fame. Wallace was agog:

> She was about four foot six and eighty-five pounds. She hit the hell out of the ball and never missed and never choked and had bad braces and pigtails that swung wildly around as she handed pros their asses. She was the first real child star in women's tennis, and in the late Seventies she was prodigious, beautiful, and inspiring. There was an incongruously adult genius about her game, all the more radiant for her little-girl giggle and silly hair. I remember meditating, with all the intensity a fifteen-year-old can summon, on the differences that kept this girl and me on our respective sides of the TV screen. She was a genius and I was not. How must it have felt? I had some serious questions to ask her. I wanted, very much, her side of it.

He gets her side of it, or some sanitized version of it, when her ghostwritten memoir appears many years later. But the memoir is so filled with cliché, so wooden and conventional, that he decides to take her down. Wallace is a genius, too, at his chosen craft of writing. Austin has wandered onto his terrain and grossly disrespected his art. She has treated it dishonestly. He takes himself to be acting on behalf of the reader. Far from being bought off with clichés, the reader wants an honest accounting of her motives and feelings. But so "clueless" is the narrator of this memoir that honesty only leaks out a little bit around the edges of a stiffly repressed and corseted "I":

> She protests, for instance, repeatedly and with an almost Gertrudian fervor, that her mother "did not force" her into tennis at age three, it apparently never occurring to Tracy Austin that a three-year-old hasn't got enough awareness of choices to require any forcing. This was the child of a mom who'd spent the evening before Tracy's birth hitting tennis balls to the family's other four children, three of whom also ended up playing pro tennis. Many of the memoir's recollections of Mrs. Austin seem almost Viennese in their repression—"My mother always made sure I behaved on court, but I never even considered acting up"—and downright creepy are some of the details Austin chooses in order to evince "how nonintense my tennis background really was":
>
>> Everyone thinks every young tennis player is very one-dimensional, which just wasn't true in my case. Until I was fourteen, I never played tennis on Monday. . . . My mother made sure I never put in seven straight days on the court. She didn't go to the club on Mondays, so we never went there.

It gets weirder. Later in the book's childhood section, Austin discusses her "wonderful friendship" with a man from their country club who "set up . . . matches for me against unsuspecting foes in later years and . . . won a lot of money from his friends" and, as a token of friendship, "bought me a necklace with a T hanging on it. The T had fourteen diamonds on it." She was apparently ten at this point. As the book's now fully adult Austin analyzes the relationship, "He was a very wealthy criminal lawyer, and I didn't have very much money. With all his gifts for me, he made me feel special." What a guy.[31]

Austin (and her ghost writer) drag out the most hackneyed narrative types: "the ingénue heroine whose innocence is eroded by experience and transcended through sheer grit," "the gruff but tender-hearted coach and the coolly skeptical veterans who finally accept the heroine," "the wicked, backstabbing rival," and "the myth-requisite humble roots" (that seem to be wholly fictional).[32] What she thereby misses, and what Wallace sees, is that her life has been tragic. She trained so hard, with such focus, that she suffered a rash of stress and overuse injuries. She peaked at seventeen and retired from the game at twenty-one:

> The only thing Tracy Austin had ever known how to do, her art—what the tragic-savvy Greeks would have called her *technë*, that state in which Austin's mastery of craft facilitated a communion with the gods themselves—was removed from her at an age when most of us are just starting to think seriously about committing ourselves to some pursuit.[33]

Wallace often writes about his own point of view. He makes no pretense to being objective about his topic; the real story is often his own subjective impressions of the person he is writing about, which makes the paradox of writing about Tracy Austin even more intense for him. He's fascinated by how she can act without thinking. Is she "an idiot or a mystic or both and/or neither"? He wants access to her inner life, which she refuses to supply. So he muscles into her territory and supplies the story she is incapable of writing. He ends on a note of triumphant reconciliation, the former opponents harmonizing together in doubles-like mutuality:

> It may well be that we spectators, who are not divinely gifted as athletes, are the only ones able truly to see, articulate, and animate the experience of the gift we are denied. And that those who receive and act out the gift of athletic genius must, perforce, be blind and dumb about it—and not because blindness and dumbness are the price of the gift, but because they are its essence.[34]

Athletic genius is blind and dumb; artistic genius sees its role as giving eyes and a voice.

Let us end with an image from Annie Dillard, a contemporary follower of Thoreau. It can stand as a living answer to all of the questions we have pursued in this book. Dillard has described her writing as a living instrument that makes its own path by the very act of traveling down it. Her image could stand for the path that the contemplative person is asked to carve out for him or herself—a box canyon at the end of the path, not clear, but we attend:

> WHEN YOU WRITE, you lay out a line of words. The line of words is a miner's pick, a woodcarver's gouge, a surgeon's probe. You wield it, and it digs a path you follow. Soon you

find yourself deep in new territory. Is it a dead end, or have you located the real subject? You will know tomorrow, or this time next year. You make the path boldly and follow it fearfully. You go where the path leads. At the end of the path, you find a box canyon. You hammer out reports, dispatch bulletins. The writing has changed, in your hands, and in a twinkling, from an expression of your notions to an epistemological tool. The new place interests you because it is not clear. You attend.[35]

Conclusion
The University and the World

This book began in the university, when we launched a class that allowed us to explore the long debate over the active and the contemplative lives, and it will end in it, since no institution better illustrates this long debate and its lasting consequences. Despite the many demographic, economic, and intellectual changes that are being forced on them, universities resist change with a special tenacity. This makes them ideal laboratories for examining the collision of past and present, as if dinosaurs and humans could be made, in a controlled setting, to occupy the same temporal realm.

Universities preserve tradition, but they also disguise and uphold social formations that other sectors can imagine to be buried in the antique past, such as class. Americans cherish the notion that higher education is a pure meritocracy that confers social mobility on talented individuals, so to insist that universities actually reinforce class difference—as many social scientists now do—is to court heresy. Yet earlier generations saw producing and preserving class difference as one of the university's key functions. Recall David Snedden in the early twentieth century, with his matter-of-fact distinction between vocational, utilitarian education for the "rank and file" and liberal education for "society's leaders." The modern university was created to produce a class-differentiated society, and the reproduction of class is written into its charters and continues to structure our institutions today. For example, the California Master Plan of 1960 was rightly hailed for its aim to provide Californians near-universal access to higher education. But it codified its educational purposes and social goals following a rigid model of class distinction. The plan's authors explain their vision with a matter-of-factness that reflects the certainties of the era: "The values of division of labor are widely recognized—in the home, in the labor force, and among the nations of the world." Following this logic, the plan differentiates three sectors of higher education according to their primary responsibilities in maintaining social division: community colleges were created for "technical curriculums, the state colleges for occupational curriculums, and the University of California for graduate and professional education and research."[1]

Clark Kerr, the architect of the master plan, drew a line between elite and non-elite universities that served, he believed, a larger social purpose. Research universities were to generate an "aristocracy of talent" that was needed "in a society increasingly based upon high knowledge and high skills," while the less selective comprehensive universities served "the labor market requirements of a modern industrial society."[2] For Kerr, this division between sectors made sense because it aligned student aptitude (as it was then understood) with educational resources and professional outcomes: the best students (the "aristocracy") would receive the best education public money could fund. For the rest (the laborers), something less could suffice. This stratified division of university sectors and students—explained by analogy to the sexual division of labor "in the home"—takes on an uncomfortable edge today, when those who enroll in selective research universities are far more likely to hail from the top 1 percent of income-earning families than from lower income brackets. In 1960 the division of higher education into a three-tiered hierarchy reflected the structure of the society it was meant to serve, with its professional, occupational, and technical tiers. But what then looked like distinctions of "aptitude" are now better understood to be distinctions of class, distinctions that are reinforced by the better funding of schools in wealthier neighborhoods and of the research universities intended (both in the original master plan and today) to serve Kerr's "artistocracy."

The division of labor that structured the 1960 California Master Plan is far less relevant in today's post-industrial economy, where the infusion of technology at all levels has collapsed distinctions between, for example, technical and professional education. The need for practical skills and training today is no more confined to the supposedly lower tiers than the need for liberal education is to the upper. Moreover, we now know more about how students learn. It was once believed that the resource-intensive education offered by research institutions, with their small classes and hands-on opportunities, would be wasted on all but a privileged few; but it's now clear that underserved and first-generation college students, long channeled toward "teaching-oriented" institutions, show the greatest gains when they're involved in research and challenged in smaller classes. Conversely, many of the pedagogical innovations that were pioneered and refined in broad-access institutions—like learning communities and online teaching—are now reinvigorating the teaching missions of selective and research-oriented institutions. Today's universities are more likely to proclaim missions of "inclusive excellence" than those of their industrial founders. Yet they maintain the forms, rituals, and core ideologies of an earlier, class-bound age.

The class-bound divisions that structured the modern university appeal to—and could be easily mistaken for—a timeless split between contemplation and action. Recall Kerr's distinction between the "technical curriculums" and "occupational curriculums" of the community colleges and comprehensive universities and the "graduate and professional education and research" of the exclusive University of California. The teaching orientation of the former (built to deliver practical "curriculums") is explicitly set against the latter's rarefied "research." With less overt class claims, universities today continue to privilege the intellectual pursuit of research over the applied labor of teaching, in a hierarchy that persists not only across the universities but within them. Even after the Carnegie Foundation stopped distinguishing "research" from "teaching" institutions in its rankings, the Carnegie classification of "R1" (research-intensive university) continues to be coveted and claimed as a marker of value, not simply of function and mission. And on many campuses, active research faculty receive considerably higher salaries, status, and social capital than do faculty who teach (there is an implicit gender distinction as well), signaling to the campus and its students that research and teaching are distinct, and hierarchically ordered, activities.

A division of academic labor also persists between administrators and faculty. Administrators are frequently caricatured as mere functionaries and bureaucrats, while the contemplative faculty are in turn caricatured (by administrators, among others) as leisured, idealistic, and lacking in practical skill or perspective. The caricatures borrow from the time-honored conventions of the active life/contemplative life debate, but the division is also reinforced by the two groups' sharply differentiated responsibilities, which leave each cut off from, and consequently mystified by, the work of the other.

As we have seen throughout this book, we make sense of the

Acknowledgments

Many people helped bring this book into the world. We were lucky to work with a group of highly talented and dedicated teaching fellows in Introduction to Humanites (IHUM), where we taught our class: Sarah Allison, Magdalena Barerra, Jennifer Barker, Bo Earle, Melissa Ganz, Abigail Heald, Christine Holbo, Ruth Kaplan, Zena Meadowsong, Christine McBride, and Melissa Stevenson. Thank you also to Russell Berman and Ellen Woods for running such excellent programs in freshman education at Stanford, including IHUM, and for encouraging us to teach this course and to make it better over the years. Ryan Johnson and Anita Law provided indispensable practical and editorial help with the manuscript. Finally, we are very grateful to Alan Thomas for his dedicated work, vision, and patience in seeing this book through from beginning to end.

Notes

Introduction

1. Although popularly attributed to Aesop, the fable probably belongs to the fifth-century Greek fabulist Avianus. This history is covered in greater depth in chapter 4.

2. Chua, *Battle Hymn of the Tiger Mother.*

3. During, "Stop Hyping Academic Freedom."

4. Aristotle, *Nicomachean Ethics,* 163.

5. We are grateful to Shane Duarte for this formulation (personal communication to BV, October 2015).

6. Aristotle, *Nicomachean Ethics,* bk. 5.

7. Milton, "L'Allegro," lines 118, 40; "Il Penseroso," lines 61, 54.

8. Milton, *Prose,* 461.

9. Plato, *Gorgias,* 56.

10. Milton, "Il Penseroso," line 174.

11. Milton, Sonnet 19, "When I Consider How My Light Is Spent."

12. Brooks, "Marshmallows and Public Policy."

13. Metcalfe and Mischel, "Hot/Cool–System Analysis," 16.

14. Campbell and Corns, *John Milton,* 29.

15. Rushkoff, *Present Shock,* 2.

16. Seneca, *Letters from a Stoic,* 35.

17. Kivetz and Keinan, "Repenting Hyperopia," 238.

18. Carnevale, Rose, and Cheah, "College Payoff."

19. Jaschik, "Obama vs. Art History."

20. "IBM 2010 Global CEO Study: Creativity Selected as Most Crucial Factor for Future Success," May 18, 2010, https://www-03.ibm

.com/press/us/en/pressrelease/31670.wss." See also Hart Research Associates, "It Takes More Than a Major."

21. "The Henry D. Thoreau Log September 1847/Walden Woods," in Thoreau, *Correspondence*.

22. Richardson, *Henry Thoreau*, 87.

23. Though Oberlin College, which served female and African American students, opened in 1833, the first institutions specifically to serve women and African Americans were both founded in 1837, the year of Thoreau's graduation: Mt. Holyoke College and Cheyney University.

24. Zajonc, personal correspondance, August 15, 2012.

25. See, for example, Lessing, "On Not Winning the Nobel Prize."

26. Montaigne, *Complete Essays*, 183.

27. Menand, *Marketplace of Ideas*, 56.

Chapter 1

1. The work of Madeline Levine has been instrumental in identifying this problem; see her *Price of Privilege* and *Teach Your Children Well*.

2. Bruni, "Best, Brightest—and Saddest?"

3. Damon, quoted in Lobdell, "Driven to Succeed."

4. Damon, *Path to Purpose*, 14.

5. Joel Elkes, quoted in Wallis, "Stress," 52.

6. Selye, *Stress of Life*, 420.

7. Selye, *Stress without Distress*, 102.

8. Selye, *From Dream to Discovery*, 9.

9. Benson, *Relaxation Response*, 150, 27.

10. James, *Varieties of Religious Experience* (1902), quoted in Benson, *Relaxation Response*, 109.

11. According to Plato, older men "who have distinguished themselves in every action of their lives and in every branch of knowledge" earn the right to "raise the eye of the soul to the universal light which lightens all things, and behold the absolute good . . . making philosophy their chief pursuit, but, when their turn comes, each devoting himself to the hard duties of public life and holding office, not as a desirable but as an unavoidable occupation." *Republic*, 540.

12. Cicero, *De Officiis*, bk. 1, sec. 43.

13. Arendt, *Human Condition*, 91.

14. Augustine, *City of God*, bk. 19, chap. 19, 881.

15. Gregory, *Homilies*, 287–88.

16. Gregory, *Morals*, 357.

17. Gregory, "Homilies 2.2.15," 77.

18. Petrarch, *De Vita Solitaria*, 290.

19. Thomas Sprat, *History of the Royal Science Society* (1667) quoted in Hunter, *Science and Society*, 87.

20. Evelyn, *Publick Employment* (London, 1667), 77, 78; quoted in Vickers, "Public and Private Life."

21. Arendt, *Human Condition*, 305–6.

22. Pope, *Doing School*, 4.

23. Sapolsky, "This Is Your Brain on Metaphors."

Chapter 2

1. Didion, *Slouching towards Bethlehem*, 30–31.

2. See *Cheney's Law*, a 2008 episode of the PBS series *Frontline*, written and directed by Michael Kirk.

3. Deresiewicz, "America's Sentimental Regard."

4. Peters and Waterman, *In Search of Excellence*, 120.

5. Thoreau, *Walden*, 5, 7.

6. Crawford, *Shop Class as Soulcraft*, 4–5, 8.

7. Ibid., 9.

8. Emerson, *Essential Writings*, 16.

9. See, as an example, the work of Rose Tarlow, a highly successful Los Angeles interior designer.

10. Crawford, *Shop Class as Soulcraft*, 181.

11. Emerson, *Essential Writings*, 319.

12. Arendt, *Human Condition*, 192.

13. Ibid., 246–47.

14. Emerson, *Essential Writings*, 229.

15. Arendt, *Human Condition*, 305–6.

16. "Arendt's title for the book, *The Human Condition*," writes one scholar, "stresses the conditioned nature of humanity in contrast to the way in which totalitarian ideologies construe of their leaders as unconditioned and all powerful beings that can control the processes of history and nature." Fry, *Arendt*, 41.

17. Arendt, *Human Condition*, 11.

18. Ibid., 302, 91.

19. We are grateful to Monika Greenleaf for this point.

20. Arendt, "Martin Heidegger at Eighty."

21. Fry, *Arendt*, 35.

22. Johnson and Boswell, *Journey to the Western Islands*, 104.

23. Wolf, "Data-Driven Life."

24. Watters, *Crazy Like Us*, 3–4.

25. Ibid., 6.

26. Siddique and Pidd, "Anders Behring Breivik Trial."

27. French, "Korea's Real Rage."

28. Cohen, "Art of the Save."

29. Gilovich, *How We Know What Isn't So*, 26.

30. Kahneman and Renshon, "Why Hawks Win."

31. Langer, "Illusion of Control," 311.

32. Ibid., 312.

33. Whitson and Galinsky, "Lacking Control," 115.

34. Ibid., 116.

35. Ibid., 117.

36. Ibid., 116.

37. Proulx, Heine, and Vohs, "When Is the Unfamiliar the Uncanny?" 817.

38. Vedantam, *Hidden Brain*, 239–40.

39. Arendt, *Human Condition*, 247.

40. Ibid., 184.

Chapter 3

1. Nor is it always as amiable. In "The World of the Intellectual vs. the World of the Engineer," a 2011 article in *Wired*, Timothy Ferris describes the two camps as those committed to "big, pretentious ideas untethered to facts," and those responsible for "the greatest increases in knowledge, health, wealth, and happiness in all human history."

2. Aurini, *Worthless*.

3. Fish, "Will the Humanities Save Us?"

4. This discussion is indebted to the work of our colleague Andrea Wilson Nightingale in *Spectacles of Truth in Classical Greek Philosophy*.

5. Aristotle, *Aristotle's Protrepticus*, sec. B41.

6. Marx, "Theses on Feuerbach," 143.

7. Blumenberg, *Legitimacy of the Modern Age*, 232, 234; see also Dickey, "Blumenberg and Secularization"; Brient, *Immanence of the Infinite*; Arendt, *Human Condition*, 305, 291.

8. Cicero, *De Officiis*, bk. 1, sec. 19. This was a favored text among English humanists arguing in favor of the active life; see Catherine Anna Louise Jarrott's "English Humanists' Use of Cicero's *De Officiis*," which examines Cicero's centrality to humanist defenses of the *vita activa*.

9. Vives, *On Education*, 284, 283. See Kahn, "Coluccio Salutati."

10. On this point, see Harrison, "Fashioned Image of Poetry."

11. As Howard Marchitello observes, early Stuart "science" was "still embedded within a range of cultural practices" and thus not "an already autonomous feature of early modernity." "Science Studies," 345.

12. Evelyn, "Letter to Robert Boyle."

13. Boyle is cited and discussed in Shapin, "House of Experiment," 386. See also Shapin, "Personal Development."

14. On the two works, see Vickers, "Public and Private Life."

15. Evelyn, *Publick Employment*, 77, 78, 115.

16. Ibid., 119.

17. Hunter, *Science and Society*, 131.

18. John Greenwood, writing to John Houghton, quoted ibid., 90.

19. Ibid., 107.

20. See Hunter, who observes "that the stress on utility had an element of public relations, emphasis on likely tangible benefits being intended to justify broader intellectual concerns to a hostile public." Ibid., 90.

21. Ibid., 29, 31.

22. Blake, *Milton a Poem*, 271.

23. Harvard Committee, *General Education in a Free Society* (Cambridge, MA: Harvard University Press, 1945), 59.

24. Ibid., 24.

25. Ibid., 17.

26. In Kallendorf, *Humanist Educational Treatises*, 105.

27. Goulding, "Humanism and Science," 233.

28. Kallendorf, *Humanist Educational Treatises*, 54, 145, 21.

29. Ibid., 14, 19.

30. Ibid., 66.

31. Ibid., vii–viii.

32. Ibid., 28. Citing Aristotle, Kallendorf defines "practical wisdom" as "prudential knowledge . . . [that is the] equivalent to moral philosophy" (167n109).

33. Aristotle, *Nicomachean Ethics* (trans. Ross), 1139b–1140b.

34. Vives, *On Education*, 284.

35. The humanities' self-imposed divorce of *epistêmê* and *technê* is attested strikingly in North American departments of English, for example, which have divided into competing areas (and sometimes distinct academic units) of literature and rhetoric, with contrastingly epistemic and technical aims.

36. Randel, "Public Good," 11.

37. Anthony T. Kronman juxtaposes the two when he asserts, "Only the recollection of humanity is an adequate response to the meaninglessness that haunts our technical powers," and calls for a "reaffirmation of the human condition that technology obscures." *Education's End*, 237. In contrast, see Alan Liu's call for a return of *technê* to the humanities in the form of technique: rather than assume that "skill" is a merely elementary toolkit and technicity "extrinsic to serious humanistic study," he asks us to consider the "possibility that there can be something deeply humane, and historically aware, about technique." *Laws of Cool*, 307.

38. Feldman, *Nobel Prize*, 146–47.

39. Clarke and Primo, *Model Discipline*.

40. Krishnan, "What Are Academic Disciplines?" 49.

41. See Crick, "Impact of Molecular Biology."

42. See the website of the National Center for Education Statistics, within the US Department of Education and the Institute of Educational Sciences, particularly the page for its Integrated Postsecondary Education Data System, https://nces.ed.gov/ipeds/.

43. This shift has been influentially described in *The New Production of Knowledge*, in which Michael Gibbons and his coauthors chart a movement from "Mode 1," a disciplinary model of knowledge production, to "Mode 2," an application-based production of knowledge that is fundamentally transdisciplinary and integrative.

44. Davies, Fidler, and Marina, "Future Work Skills 2020," 11.

45. Ibid.

46. Emerson, *Essential Writings*, 319; Center for Information Technology Research in the Interest of Society (CITRIS) website, accessed August 10, 2012, http://citris-uc.org/.

47. Thomas and Brown, *New Culture of Learning*.

48. Tapscott, *Grown Up Digital*, 142.

49. Thomas and Brown, *New Culture of Learning*.

50. Hansen, "Imagination."

51. Shepherd, "Fertile Minds Need Feeding." "The powers of creative thinking," Robinson insists, are "some of the most important capacities that young people now need to make their way in the increasingly demanding world of the 21st century"—yet current approaches to education more often stifle than stimulate them.

52. Dewey, *Democracy and Education*, 334, 302.

53. Hutchins, *Higher Learning in America*, 32.

54. Eliot, "Urban University," 396.

55. Webster, "Aristocracy of Achievement," 174–75.

56. Labaree, "How Dewey Lost," 165. The following discussion also draws on Ravitch, *Left Back*, and Kliebard, *Struggle for the American Curriculum*.

57. Snedden, "What of Liberal Education?"

58. Snedden, cited in Ravitch, *Left Back*, 83; Snedden, "Schools of Rank and File," 189.

59. Snedden, "Schools of Rank and File," 195.

60. Snedden, *Vocational Education*, 95; Labaree, "How Dewey Lost," 175; 178.

61. Ravitch, *Left Back*, 85.

62. Kliebard, *Struggle for the American Curriculum*, 119.

63. Labaree, "How Dewey Lost," 184.

64. Kliebard, *Schooled to Work*, 120. In *Struggle for the American Curriculum*, Kliebard observes, "Social utility became the supreme criterion against which the value of school studies was measured" (78).

65. Snedden, "Cardinal Principles," 519.

66. Dewey, "Democratic Faith," 233.

67. Ibid.

68. Dewey, *Quest for Certainty*, 17; 19.

69. Dewey, *Democracy and Education*, 306.

70. Ibid., 358.

71. Dewey, *Quest for Certainty*, 79.

72. Ibid., 167.

73. Dewey, *Reconstruction in Philosophy*, 16. Alan Ryan refers to "Dewey's hero Francis Bacon" in his biography *John Dewey and the High Tide of American Liberalism* (232).

74. Bacon, "Letter to Isaac Casaubon," in *Major Works*, xx.

75. Bacon, *Major Works*, 150.

76. Ibid., 244–45.

77. Dewey, *Democracy and Education*, 358, 298.

78. Ibid., 300.

79. Dewey, *Quest for Certainty*, 220.

80. Ibid., 220–21.

81. Ibid., 251.

82. Dewey, *Democracy and Education*, 338.

83. Dewey, *Educational Situation*, 87–88, 89.

84. Schneider, "Liberal Education," 3.

85. Colby et al., *Rethinking Undergraduate Business Education*. 51.

86. Ibid., 68.

87. Ibid.

88. See the essays in Orrill, *Education and Democracy*.

89. Berry, "Loss of the University," 77. This passage appears as the epigraph to Palmer, Zajonc, and Scribner, *Heart of Higher Education*, which relates examples of campuses that align with Berry's call and inspired us to invite one of its authors, Arthur Zajonc, to speak to our class.

90. In Kallendorf, *Humanist Educational Treatises*, 83.

91. Kristeller, *Renaissance Thought*, 98. As James Hankins observes, "The humanists claimed that study of good letters made people better, more virtuous, wiser, and more eloquent. It made them worthy to exercise power and made them better citizens and subjects when not exercising power. Humane studies embellished life, brought pleasure, and nourished piety." "Humanism, Scholasticism, and Renaissance Philosophy," 32. Christopher Celenza makes a similar point: "To be 'humane' (*humanus*) meant not only to be a human being but also to have exercised one's capacity as a human being to the fullest through learning." "Humanism and the Classical Tradition," 27.

Chapter 4

1. Bauerlein, "What's the Point of a Professor?"

2. "The Unexamined but Affluent Life," *Chicago Tribune*, February 27, 2004, http://articles.chicagotribune.com/2004-02-27/news/04022 70314_1_college-freshmen-philosophy-ucla-study.

3. Eagan et al., "American Freshman: National Norms" (2016); compared to Astin et al., "American Freshman: National Norms" (1986), and Panos et al., "National Norms" (1967), 50.

4. Pryor et al., "American Freshman: Forty Year Trends," 33.

5. Eagan et al., "American Freshman: National Norms," 47.

6. Ibid., 44; Pryor et al., "American Freshman: Forty Year Trends," 33.

7. Veblen, *Theory of the Leisure Class*, 33.

8. Pieper, *Leisure*, 38, 46.

9. De Grazia, *Of Time, Work, and Leisure*, 413.

10. Pieper, *Leisure*, 51; De Grazia, *Of Time, Work, and Leisure*, 377–78.

11. Mills, *White Collar*, 237.

12. Bolles, *What Color Is Your Parachute?* 91–92.

13. Bronson, *What Should I Do with My Life?* 11–12; 43; 12, 37, 55; 15; 17; 26; 13.

14. De Botton, *Pleasures and Sorrows of Work*, 30.

15. Tan, *Search inside Yourself*, 139; 134.

16. Chafkin, "Oracle of Silicon Valley."

17. Tan, *Search inside Yourself*, 3.

18. Schumacher, *Good Work*, 119, 122.

19. Winograd and Hais, *Millennial Momentum*, 139, 141.

20. Malone, *Future of Work*, 41, 55.

21. Williams and Tapscott, *Wikinomics*.

22. Lerer, *Children's Literature*.

23. La Fontaine, *Complete Fables*, 5.

24. For a survey of versions, see Perry, *Aesopica*. The fable's textual history has been traced by Francisco Rodriguez Adrados in *History of the Graeco-Latin Fable* and *Inventory and Documentation of the Graeco-Latin Fable*.

25. Perry, *Aesopica*, 112.

26. Desmond and Gerrard, *Cynics*, 102.

27. Hesiod, *Works and Days*, lines 300–312.

28. Aristophanes, *The Clouds*, discussed in Lis, "Perceptions of Work," 36.

29. De France, *Fables*, 119.

30. L'Estrange et al., *Fables of Aesop*, 190, 189.

31. Bewick, *Fables of Aesop*, 130–31.

32. L'Estrange et al., *Fables of Aesop*, preface.

33. Rosenzwig, *Eight Hours for What We Will*, 1.

34. Rybczynski, *Waiting for the Weekend*.

35. Thompson, "Time, Work-Discipline, and Industrial Capitalism," 90.

36. Fisher, "Bright Perilous Face of Leisure"; Pound, "Out of Unemployment into Leisure"; Coffin, "Too Little Culture for Leisure"; Finley, "What Will We Do with Our Time?" See Hunnicutt, *Work without End*.

37. Pack, *Challenge of Leisure*, 58.

38. "The Big Bad Wolf," *Fortune*, November 1934, 89–95, 142–48; 89.

39. Ibid., 88.

40. Ibid., 146, 145.

41. Ibid., 89.

42. These treasures of early advertising are archived in "Gallery of Graphic Design," accessed February 22, 2014, http://graphic-design.tjs-labs.com/table-view.php?year=1934. See also Lears, *Fables of Abundance*, 237.

43. "Big Bad Wolf," 93.

44. "*Frederick*—Customer Reviews," accessed November 15, 2015, http://www.amazon.com/Frederick-Leo-Lionni/product-reviews/0394826140/

45. Mills, *White Collar*, xvi, 237.

46. Levine, *Price of Privilege*, 158.

47. Isaacson, *Steve Jobs*, 240.

48. Schlender, "Lost Steve Jobs Tapes."

49. McGrath and MacDermott, "Andrew Stanton," 117.

50. Paik, *To Infinity and Beyond!* 125.

51. McGrath and MacDermott, "Andrew Stanton," 114; 117.

52. Paik, *To Infinity and Beyond!* 131.

53. Gunther and Vinzant, "Eisner's Mousetrap."

54. Stewart, *Disney War*, 90.

55. Isaacson, *Steve Jobs*, 437.

56. Gordon, *Ant Encounters*. The summary comes from the publisher's website, accessed March 24, 2016, http://press.princeton.edu/titles/9240.html.

57. Castells, *Rise of the Network Society*, 1:3; 17–18.

58. De Grazia, *Of Time, Work, and Leisure*, 413; Mills, *White Collar*, 237.

59. Karnes, *Imagination, Meditation, and Cognition*.

60. Thomas Aquinas, *Philosophical Texts*, Opusc. IX, Exposition de Hebdomadibus, pt. Prologue.

61. Suits, *Grasshopper*, 149.

62. Schumacher, *Good Work*, 122.

Chapter 5

1. Maloney and Fujikawa, "Marie Kondo and the Cult of Tidying Up"; Parry, "Marie Kondo Is the Maiden of Mess."

2. Kondō, *Life-Changing Magic*, 177, 171.

3. Ibid., 188.

4. Parry, "Marie Kondo Is the Maiden of Mess."

5. Kondō, *Life-Changing Magic*, 64.

6. Bender, *Plain and Simple*, 145.

7. Ibid., 90.

8. Matchar, *Homeward Bound*.

9. Ibid., 25; 239.

10. McKeon, *Secret History of Domesticity*, 9.

11. Parry, "Marie Kondo Is the Maiden of Mess."

12. Bender, *Plain and Simple*, 138.

13. Ibid., 50, 51.

14. Taylor, *Secular Age*, 380, 5.

15. Ibid., 2, 179.

16. Thomas à Kempis, *Imitation of Christ*, 30.

17. Philo, *On Mating*, 489; 471.

18. Philo, *Posterity and Exile*, 407.

19. Dresner, *Rachel*, 53.

20. Augustine, *Answer to Faustus*, 1:336.

21. Luke 10:38–42, Confraternity-Douay Version.

22. Augustine, *Sermons*, 1:420.

23. Ernst, *Martha from the Margins*, 184–85; Fiorenza, "Feminist Critical Interpretation," 30; Seim, "Gospel of Luke," 745–46.

24. Origen, *Homilies on Luke*, 215.

25. Hochstrasser, *Still Life and Trade*, 1.

26. Carducho, *Dialogos de la Pintura* (1633), quoted in Casal, "Old Woman"; Moxey, "Erasmus."

27. This point is consistent with Messalian interpretations of Martha as a representative of work per se: see Ernst, *Martha from the Margins*, 220–21.

28. Byatt, *Elementals*, 226–27.

29. Pfeiffer, "Good Housewife," sec. 52, 134.

30. Teresa, *Complete Works*, 3:22.

31. Shulevitz, *Sabbath World*, xxiii.

32. Ibid., 88.

33. Heschel, *Sabbath*, 19.

34. Philo, *De Specialibus Legibus*, 7:347.

35. *The Sabbath Manifesto* calls for new principles that honor the spirit of the Sabbath, such as "avoid technology" and "avoid commerce." Kondō, *Life-Changing Magic*, 64.

36. Heschel, *Sabbath*, 19.

37. Kondō, *Life-Changing Magic*, 61.

38. Tyler, *Primitive Culture*, 385.

39. Ibid., 431.

40. Kingsolver et al., *Animal, Vegetable, Miracle*, 20.

41. Ibid., 67.

42. Ibid., 124.

43. Ibid., 308.

44. Ibid., 309, 308.

45. Ibid., 39, 133.

46. Ibid., 284.

47. Taylor, *Secular Age*, 507.

48. Weich, "Barbara Kingsolver Does Something Great."

49. Kingsolver, *Poisonwood Bible*, 38, 41.

50. Ibid., 520, 522.

51. Ibid., 525, 522.

52. Ibid., 514.

53. Ibid., 516.

54. Ibid., 516, 429, 519.

55. Kingsolver et al., *Animal, Vegetable, Miracle*, 5,

56. Ibid., 18.

Chapter 6

1. Paris, "George Eliot's Religion of Humanity," 419.

2. Eliot, *Middlemarch*.

3. Eliot, *Journals*, 325.

4. Eliot, *George Eliot's Life*, 348. Ironically, anybody who has read *Middlemarch* knows that the book's narrator is perfectly capable of preaching. In fact, one of the striking experiences of reading the book is being hectored, if not bullied, by a sadistic narrator.

5. Eliot, *Middlemarch*, 215.

6. Ibid., 115.

7. Ashton, *George Eliot*, vi.

8. Eliot, *Middlemarch*, 96-97.

9. Rodham, "1969 Student Commencement Speech."

10. This point belongs to Alexander Welsh's *George Eliot and Blackmail*.

11. Ibid.

12. Boyle, "Theory of Law and Information," 1485. He continues: "This belief is given a particular 'spin' by our practice, within that sphere, of defining the norm of justified protection largely by reference to the right to withhold and control information. Intuitively, blackmail seems like the intrusion of market logic into the realm that should be most 'private.' To put it another way, we do not think that we should commodify relationships in the private realm. To commodify is itself to violate the private realm."

13. Welsh, *George Eliot and Blackmail*, 131.

14. Iyengar and Lepper, "When Choice Is Demotivating."

15. Sunstein and Ullmann-Margalit, "Second-Order Decisions."

16. Schwartz, *Paradox of Choice*, chap. 2.

17. Ibid., 132.

18. Eliot, *Middlemarch*, 486.

19. Miller, *Narrative and Its Discontents*, 179.

20. Kafka, *Diaries*, 222.

21. Locke, *Works*, 740.

22. Siegel, *Mindsight*, x.

23. Thoreau, *Journal*, 68.

24. Crespi and Badcock, "Psychosis and Autism," 261–320.

25. Eliot, *George Eliot's Life*, 52.

26. Didion, *Year of Magical Thinking*, 144.

27. Wallace, *Consider the Lobster*, 154.

28. Milton et al., "Mind of Expert Motor Performance," 808.

29. This is a standing joke in British comedy. See, e.g., Spiegl, *Game of Two Halves, Brian*. Thank you to Simon Firth for the reference.

30. Bascom, "Brainy Ballplayers."

31. Wallace, *Consider the Lobster*.

32. Ibid., 145.

33. Ibid., 150.

34. Ibid., 155.

35. Dillard, *Writing Life*, 3.

Conclusion

1. Coons et al., "Master Plan," 34, 35.

2. Kerr, "California Master Plan," 47–60.

3. Drucker and Maciariello, *Management*, 522; 517.

4. Graham, "Maker's Schedule, Manager's Schedule," July 2009, http://www.paulgraham.com/makersschedule.html; MacKay, "Can We Be Both Makers and Managers?"

5. Mason, *Postcapitalism*, xvii.

Bibliography

Adrados, Francisco Rodriguez. *History of the Graeco-Latin Fable*. Vol. 2, *The Fable during the Roman Empire and in the Middle Ages*. Translated by Nicholas Dylan Ray and Leslie A. Ray. Leiden: Brill, 2000.

———. *Inventory and Documentation of the Graeco-Latin Fable*. Translated by Gert-Jan van Dijk. Leiden: Brill, 2003.

Arendt, Hannah. *The Human Condition*. 2nd ed. Chicago: University of Chicago Press, 1998.

———. "Martin Heidegger at Eighty." Translated by Albert Hofstadter. *New York Review of Books*, October 21, 1971. http://www.nybooks.com/articles/1971/10/21/martin-heidegger-at-eighty/.

Aristotle. *Aristotle's Protrepticus: An Attempt at Reconstruction*. Edited by Ingemar Düring. Göteborg: Elanders Boktryckeri Aktiebolag, 1961.

———. *Nicomachean Ethics*. Translated by David Ross. Oxford: Oxford University Press, 2009.

———. *Nicomachean Ethics*. Translated by Terence Irwin. Indianapolis: Hackett, 1985.

Ashton, Rosemary. *George Eliot: A Life*. New York: Penguin, 1996.

Astin, Alexander W., Kenneth C. Green, William S. Korn, and Marilyn Schalit. "The American Freshman: National Norms Fall 1986." Los Angeles: Higher Education Research Institute, UCLA, 1986.

Augustine. *Answer to Faustus, a Manichean*. Translated by Roland Teske. Vol. 1 of *The Works of Saint Augustine: A Translation for the 21st Century*. Brooklyn: New City Press, 2007.

———. *The City of God*. Translated by Marcus Dods. Peabody: Hendrickson, 2009.

———. *Sermons on Selected Lessons*. 2 vols. Oxford, 1844.

Aurini, Davis. *Worthless: The Young Person's Indispensable Guide to Choosing the Right Major*. Excelsior, MN: Paric Publishing, 2011.

Bacon, Francis. *Francis Bacon: The Major Works*. Edited by Brian Vickers. Oxford: Oxford University Press, 1996.

Bascom, Nick. "Brainy Ballplayers." *Science News*, December 30, 2011. https://www.sciencenews.org/article/brainy-ballplayers.

Bauerlein, Mark. "What's the Point of a Professor?" *New York Times*, May 9, 2015. http://www.nytimes.com/2015/05/10/opinion/sunday/whats-the-point-of-a-professor.html.

Bewick, Thomas. *The Fables of Aesop, and Others*. Newcastle, 1818.

Bender, Sue. *Plain and Simple: A Woman's Journey to the Amish*. San Francisco: HarperCollins, 1989.

Benson, Herbert. *The Relaxation Response*. New York: William Morrow, 1975.

Berry, Wendell. "The Loss of the University." In *Home Economics: Fourteen Essays*. San Francisco: North Point Press, 1987.

Blake, William. *Milton a Poem, and the Final Illuminated Works: The Ghost of Abel, On Homers Poetry, [and] On Virgil Laocoön*. Edited by Robert N. Essick and Joseph Viscomi. Princeton, NJ: Princeton University Press, 1993.

Blumenberg, Hans. *The Legitimacy of the Modern Age*. Translated by Robert M. Wallace. Cambridge, MA: MIT Press, 1983.

Bolles, Richard Nelson. *What Color Is Your Parachute? A Practical Manual for Job-Hunters and Career Changers*. Berkeley, CA: Ten Speed Press, 1980.

Boyle, James. "A Theory of Law and Information: Copyright, Spleens, Blackmail, and Insider Trading." *California Law Review* 80, no. 6 (December 1992): 1413–1540.

Brient, Elizabeth. *The Immanence of the Infinite: Hans Blumenberg and the Threshold to Modernity*. Washington, DC: Catholic University of America Press, 2002.

Bronson, Po. *What Should I Do with My Life? The True Story of People Who Answered the Ultimate Question*. New York: Ballantine, 2002.

Brooks, David. "Marshmallows and Public Policy." *New York Times*,

May 7, 2006. http://www.nytimes.com/2006/05/07/opinion/07 brooks.html.

Bruni, Frank. "Best, Brightest—and Saddest?" *New York Times*, April 11, 2015. http://www.nytimes.com/2015/04/12/opinion/sunday/frank -bruni-best-brightest-and-saddest.html.

Byatt, A. S. *Elementals: Stories of Fire and Ice*. London: Chatto & Windus, 1998.

Campbell, Gordon, and Thomas N. Corns. *John Milton: Life, Work, and Thought*. Oxford: Oxford University Press, 2010.

Carnevale, Anthony P., Stephen J. Rose, and Ban Cheah. "The College Payoff: Education, Occupations, Lifetime Earnings." Georgetown University Center on Education and the Workforce, 2011. https:// repository.library.georgetown.edu/handle/10822/559300.

Casal, Marta Cacho. "The Old Woman in Velázquez's *Kitchen Scene with Christ's Visit to Martha and Mary*." *Journal of the Warburg and Courtauld Institutes*, no. 58 (2000): 295–302.

Castells, Manuel. *The Rise of the Network Society*. Vol. 1 of *The Information Age: Economy, Society, and Culture*. Malden, MA: Wiley-Blackwell, 2010.

Celenza, Christopher. "Humanism and the Classical Tradition." *Annali d'Italianistica* 26 (2008): 25–49.

Chafkin, Max. "The Oracle of Silicon Valley." *Inc.*, May 1, 2010. http:// www.inc.com/magazine/20100501/the-oracle-of-silicon-valley .html.

Chua, Amy. *Battle Hymn of the Tiger Mother*. London: Bloomsbury Paperbacks, 2012.

Cicero. *De Officiis*. Translated by George B. Gardiner. London: Methuen & Co., 1899.

Clarke, Kevin A., and David M. Primo. *A Model Discipline: Political Science and the Logic of Representations*. Oxford: Oxford University Press, 2012.

Coffin, W. S. "Too Little Culture for Leisure." *American Magazine of Art* 26, no. 6 (June 1933): 299–300.

Cohen, Patricia. "The Art of the Save, for Goalie and Investor." *New York Times*, March 1, 2008. http://www.nytimes.com/2008/03/01 /business/01kick.html.

Colby, Anne, Thomas Ehrlich, William M. Sullivan, and Jonathan R.

Dolle. *Rethinking Undergraduate Business Education: Liberal Learning for the Profession*. San Francisco: Jossey-Bass, 2011.

Coons, Arthur G., Arthur D. Browne, Howard A. Campion, Glenn S. Dumke, Thomas C. Holy, Dean E. McHenry, Henry T. Tyler, and Robert J. Wert. "A Master Plan for Higher Education in California, 1960–1975." Liaison Committee of the State Board of Education and the Regents of the University of California, 1960.

Crawford, Matthew B. *Shop Class as Soulcraft: An Inquiry into the Value of Work*. New York: Penguin, 2009.

Crespi, Bernard, and Christopher Badcock. "Psychosis and Autism as Diametrical Disorders of the Social Brain." *Behavioral and Brain Sciences* 31, no. 3 (2008): 241–61.

Crick, Francis. "The Impact of Molecular Biology on Neuroscience." *Philosophical Transactions of the Royal Society of Biological Sciences* 354, no. 1392 (December 1999): 2021–25.

Damon, William. *The Path to Purpose: How Young People Find Their Calling in Life*. New York: Free Press, 2009.

Davies, Anna, Devin Fidler, and Gorbis Marina. "Future Work Skills 2020." Palo Alto, CA: Institute for the Future for the University of Phoenix Research Institute, 2011.

De Botton, Alain. *The Pleasures and Sorrows of Work*. New York: Pantheon, 2009.

De France, Marie. *The Fables of Marie de France*. Translated by Mary Lou Martin. Birmingham, AL: Summa, 1984.

De Grazia, Sebastian. *Of Time, Work, and Leisure*. New York: Twentieth Century Fund, 1962.

Deresiewicz, William. "America's Sentimental Regard for the Military." *New York Times*, August 20, 2011. http://www.nytimes.com/2011/08/21/opinion/sunday/americas-sentimental-regard-for-the-military.html.

Desmond, William, and Steven Gerrard. *Cynics*. Berkeley: University of California Press, 2008.

Dewey, John. *Democracy and Education: An Introduction to the Philosophy of Education*. New York: Macmillan, 1916.

———. "The Democratic Faith and Education." In *John Dewey: The Essential Writings*, edited by David Sidorsky, 226–34. New York: HarperCollins, 1977.

———. *The Educational Situation*. Chicago: University Of Chicago Press, 1904.

———. *The Quest for Certainty: A Study of the Relation of Knowledge and Action*. New York: Capricorn, 1960.

———. *Reconstruction in Philosophy*. Boston: Beacon Press, 1957.

Dickey, Laurence. "Blumenberg and Secularization: 'Self-Assertion' and the Problem of Self-Realizing Teleology in History." *New German Critique* 41 (Spring–Summer 1987): 151–65. doi:10.2307/488280.

Didion, Joan. *Slouching towards Bethlehem: Essays*. New York: Farrar, Straus and Giroux, 1990.

———. *The Year of Magical Thinking*. New York: Vintage, 2007.

Dillard, Annie. *The Writing Life*. New York: Harper Perennial, 1990.

Dresner, Samuel H. *Rachel*. Minneapolis: Fortress Press, 1994.

Drucker, Peter F., and Joseph A. Maciariello. *Management*. Rev. ed. New York: Harper Business, 2008.

During, Simon. "Stop Hyping Academic Freedom." *Public Books*. Accessed December 21, 2015. http://www.publicbooks.org/nonfiction/stop-hyping-academic-freedom.

Eagan, M. K., E. B. Stolzenberg, H. B. Zimmerman, M. C. Aragon, H. Whang Sayson, and C. Rios-Aguilar. "The American Freshman: National Norms Fall 2016." Los Angeles: Higher Education Research Institute, UCLA, 2017.

Eliot, Charles William. "An Urban University." In *Educational Reform: Essays and Addresses*, 395–400. New York: Century, 1898.

Eliot, George. *George Eliot's Life, as Related in Her Letters and Journals*. Cambridge: Cambridge University Press, 2010.

———. *The Journals of George Eliot*. Edited by Margaret Harris and Judith Johnston. Rev. ed. Cambridge: Cambridge University Press, 2000.

Emerson, Ralph Waldo. *The Essential Writings of Ralph Waldo Emerson*. Edited by Brooks Atkinson. New York: Modern Library, 2000.

Ernst, Allie M. *Martha from the Margins: The Authority of Martha in Early Christian Tradition*. Boston: Brill, 2009.

Evelyn, John. "John Evelyn, Letter to Robert Boyle, 3 September 1659." In *Diary and Correspondence of John Evelyn, F.R.S. To Which Is Subjoined the Private Correspondence between King Charles I. and Sir Edward Nicholas, and between Sir Edward Hyde, Afterwards Earl of Clarendon, and Sir Richard Browne*, edited by William Bray, 3:118. London: H. Colburn & Co., 1852.

Feldman, Burton. *The Nobel Prize: A History of Genius, Controversy, and Prestige*. New York: Arcade, 2012.

Ferris, Timothy. "The World of the Intellectual vs. the World of the Engineer." *Wired*, October 13, 2011. http://www.wired.com/2011/10/intellectual-vs-engineer/.

Finley, J. H. "What Will We Do with Our Time?" *National Municipal Review* 22 (1933): 416–17.

Fiorenza, Elizabeth Schüssler. "A Feminist Critical Interpretation for Liberation: Martha and Mary, Lk. 10:38–42." *Religion and Intellectual Life* 3, no. 2 (1986): 3–79.

Fish, Stanley. "Will the Humanities Save Us?" *New York Times*, "Opinionator" blog, January 6, 2008. http://opinionator.blogs.nytimes.com/2008/01/06/will-the-humanities-save-us/.

Fisher, D. C. "The Bright Perilous Face of Leisure." *Journal of Adult Education* 5 (June 1933): 237–47.

French, Howard W. "Korea's Real Rage for Virtual Games." *New York Times*, October 9, 2002. http://www.nytimes.com/2002/10/09/world/korea-s-real-rage-for-virtual-games.html.

Fry, Karin A. *Arendt: A Guide for the Perplexed*. Guides for the Perplexed. New York: Bloomsbury Academic, 2009.

Gibbons, Michael, Camille Limoges, Helga Nowotny, Simon Schwartzman, Peter Scott, and Martin Trow. *The New Production of Knowledge: The Dynamics of Science and Research in Contemporary Societies*. Thousand Oaks, CA: Sage, 1994.

Gilovich, Thomas. *How We Know What Isn't So: The Fallibility of Human Reason in Everyday Life*. New York: Free Press, 1991.

Gordon, Deborah M. *Ant Encounters: Interaction Networks and Colony Behavior*. Princeton, NJ: Princeton University Press, 2010.

Goulding, Robert. "Humanism and Science in Elizabethan Universities." In *Reassessing Tudor Humanism*, edited by Jonathan Woolfsonm 223–42. Basingstoke: Palgrave Macmillan, 2002.

Gregory the Great. "Homilies 2.2.15." In *The Growth of Mysticism: Gregory the Great through the 12th Century*, edited by Bernard McGinn. Vol. 2 of *The Presence of God: A History of Western Christian Mysticism*. New York: Crossroad Publishing, 1999.

———. *Homilies on the Book of the Prophet Ezekiel*. Translated by Theodosia Tomkinson. Etna: Center for Traditionalist Orthodox Studies, 2008.

———. *Morals on the Book of Job*. Edited by J. H. Parker. Oxford: J. H. Parker, 1844.

Gunther, Mark, and Carol Vinzant. "Eisner's Mousetrap." *Fortune*, September 6, 1999. http://archive.fortune.com/magazines/fortune/fortune_archive/1999/09/06/265291/index.htm.

Hankins, James. "Humanism, Scholasticism, and Renaissance Philosophy." In *The Cambridge Companion to Renaissance Philosophy*, edited by James Hankins. Cambridge: Cambridge University Press, 2007.

Hansen, Drew. "Imagination: What You Need to Thrive in the Future Economy." *Forbes*, August 6, 2012. http://www.forbes.com/sites/drewhansen/2012/08/06/imagination-future-economy/.

Harrison, Peter. "'The Fashioned Image of Poetry or the Regular Instruction of Philosophy?' Truth, Utility, and the Natural Sciences in Early Modern England." In *Science, Literature and Rhetoric in Early Modern England*, edited by Juliet Cummins and David Burchell, 15–35. Aldershot: Ashgate, 2007.

Hart Research Associates. "It Takes More Than a Major: Employer Priorities for College Learning and Student Success." Association of American Colleges and Universities, April 10, 2013. http://www.aacu.org/leap/documents/2013_EmployerSurvey.pdf.

Heschel, Abraham Joshua. *The Sabbath*. New York: Farrar, Straus and Giroux, 1951.

Hesiod. *Works and Days*. Translated by Hugh G. Evelyn-White. In *Hesiod, the Homeric Hymns, and Homerica*. London: Heinemann, 1914.

Hochstrasser, Julie Berger. *Still Life and Trade in the Dutch Golden Age*. New Haven, CT: Yale University Press, 2007.

Hunnicutt, Benjamin. *Work without End: Abandoning Shorter Hours for the Right to Work*. Philadelphia: Temple University Press, 1988.

Hunter, Michael. *Science and Society in Restoration England*. Cambridge: Cambridge University Press, 1981.

Hutchins, Robert Maynard. *The Higher Learning in America*. New Haven, CT: Yale University Press, 1936.

Isaacson, Walter. *Steve Jobs: A Biography.* New York: Simon & Schuster, 2011.

Iyengar, S. S., and M. R. Lepper. "When Choice Is Demotivating: Can One Desire Too Much of a Good Thing?" *Journal of Personality and Social Psychology* 79, no. 6 (December 2000): 995–1006.

Jarrott, Catherine Anna Louise. "The English Humanists' Use of Cicero's *De Officiis* in Their Evaluation of Active and Contemplative Life." Thesis, Stanford University, 1954.

Jaschik, Scott. "Obama vs. Art History." *Inside Higher Ed*, January 31, 2014. https://www.insidehighered.com/news/2014/01/31/obama -becomes-latest-politician-criticize-liberal-arts-discipline.

Johnson, Samuel, and James Boswell. *The Journey to the Western Islands of Scotland and the Journal of a Tour to the Hebrides.* Edited by Peter Levi. New York: Penguin Classics, 1984.

Kafka, Franz. *Diaries, 1910–1923.* New York: Schocken, 1988.

Kahn, Victoria. "Coluccio Salutati on the Active and Contemplative Lives." In *Arbeit, Musse, Meditation: Betrachtungen zur "Vita Activa" und "Vita Contemplativa,"* edited by Brian Vickers, 153–80. Zürich: Verlag de Fachvereine, 1985.

Kahneman, Daniel, and Jonathan Renshon. "Why Hawks Win." *Foreign Policy*, December 27, 2006. http://www.foreignpolicy.com /articles/2006/12/27/why_hawks_win.

Kallendorf, Craig W., ed. and trans. *Humanist Educational Treatises.* Bilingual edition, with texts by Leonardo Bruni, Battista Guarino, Aeneas Silvius Piccolomini, and Pier Paolo Vergerio. Cambridge, MA: Harvard University Press, 2002.

Karnes, Michelle. *Imagination, Meditation, and Cognition in the Middle Ages.* Chicago: University of Chicago Press, 2011.

Kerr, Clark. "The California Master Plan of 1960 for Higher Education—An Ex Ante View." In *The OECD, the Master Plan and the California Dream: A Berkeley Conversation*, edited by Sheldon Rothblatt. University of California at Berkeley. Accessed March 31, 2016. http://content.cdlib.org/view?docId=hb8489p1ft.

Kingsolver, Barbara. *The Poisonwood Bible: A Novel.* New York: Harper Perennial Modern Classics, 2008.

Kingsolver, Barbara, Steven L. Hopp, Camille Kingsolver, and Richard

A Houser. *Animal, Vegetable, Miracle: A Year of Food Life*. New York: Harper, 2007.

Kivetz, Ran, and Anat Keinan. "Repenting Hyperopia: An Analysis of Self-Control Regrets." *Journal of Consumer Research* 33 (September 2006): 273–82.

Kliebard, Herbert M. *Schooled to Work: Vocationalism and the American Curriculum, 1876–1946*. New York: Teachers College Press, 1999.

———. *The Struggle for the American Curriculum, 1893–1958*. New York: Routledge, 2004.

Kondō, Marie. *The Life-Changing Magic of Tidying Up: The Japanese Art of Decluttering and Organizing*. Translated by Cathy Hirano. Berkeley, CA: Ten Speed Press, 2014.

Krishnan, Armin. "What Are Academic Disciplines? Observations on the Disciplinarity vs. Interdisciplinarity Debate." University of Southampton, Economic and Social Research Council National Centre for Research Methods Working Paper Series, 2009.

Kristeller, Paul O. *Renaissance Thought and Its Sources*. New York: Columbia University Press, 1979.

Kronman, Anthony T. *Education's End: Why Our Colleges and Universities Have Given Up on the Meaning of Life*. New Haven, CT: Yale University Press, 2008.

Labaree, David F. "How Dewey Lost: The Victory of David Snedden and Social Efficiency in the Reform of American Education." In *Pragmatism and Modernities*, edited by Daniel Tröhler, Thomas Schlag, and Fritz Osterwalder, 164–88. Boston: Sense Publishers, 2011.

La Fontaine, Jean de. *The Complete Fables of Jean de La Fontaine*. Translated by Norman B. Spector. Evanston, IL: Northwestern University Press, 1988.

Langer, Ellen J. "The Illusion of Control." *Journal of Personality and Social Psychology* 32, no. 2 (1975): 311–28.

Lears, Jackson. *Fables of Abundance: A Cultural History of Advertising in America*. New York: Basic Books, 1995.

Lerer, Seth. *Children's Literature: A Reader's History, from Aesop to Harry Potter*. Chicago: University of Chicago Press, 2009.

Lessing, Doris. "On Not Winning the Nobel Prize." Nobel Lecture,

December 7, 2007. http://www.nobelprize.org/nobel_prizes/litera
ture/laureates/2007/lessing-lecture_en.html.

L'Estrange, Roger, Adriaan van Baarland, Avianus, Lorenzo Astemio,
and Poggio Bracciolini. *Fables of Aesop and Other Eminent Mythologists with Morals and Reflexions*. London, 1692.

Levine, Madeline. *The Price of Privilege: How Parental Pressure and
Material Advantage Are Creating a Generation of Disconnected and
Unhappy Kids*. New York: HarperCollins, 2008.

———. *Teach Your Children Well: Parenting For Authentic Success*. New
York: HarperCollins, 2013.

Lis, Catharina. "Perceptions of Work in Classical Antiquity: A Poly-
phonic Heritage." In *The Idea of Work in Europe from Antiquity to
Modern Times*, edited by Josef Ehmer and Catharina Lis, 33–68.
Burlington: Ashgate, 2009.

Liu, Alan. *The Laws of Cool: Knowledge Work and the Culture of Information*. Chicago: University of Chicago Press, 2004.

Lobdell, Terri. "Driven to Succeed: How We're Depriving Teens of
a Sense of Purpose." *Palo Alto Online*, November 18, 2011. http://
www.paloaltoonline.com/news/2011/11/18/driven-to-succeed
-part-1-getting-off-the-treadmill.

Locke, John. *The Works of John Locke, Esq*. London, 1751.

MacKay, Jory. "Can We Be Both Makers and Managers?" *Observer*,
November 3, 2015. http://observer.com/2015/11/can-we-be-both
-makers-and-managers/.

Malone, Thomas W. *The Future of Work: How the New Order of Business
Will Shape Your Organization, Your Management Style and Your Life*.
Boston: Harvard Business Review Press, 2004.

Maloney, Jennifer, and Megumi Fujikawa. "Marie Kondo and the Cult
of Tidying Up." *Wall Street Journal*, February 26, 2015. http://www
.wsj.com/articles/marie-kondo-and-the-tidying-up-trend-14249
70535.

Marchitello, Howard. "Science Studies and English Renaissance Literature." *Literature Compass* 3, no. 3 (May 2006): 341–65. doi:10.
1111/j.1741-4113.2006.00318.x.

Marx, Karl. "Theses on Feuerbach." In *The Marx-Engels Reader*, edited
by Robert Tucker, 2nd rev. ed., 143–45. New York: W. W. Norton,
1979.

Mason, Paul. *Postcapitalism: A Guide to Our Future*. London: Random House, 2015.

Matchar, Emily. *Homeward Bound: Why Women Are Embracing the New Domesticity*. New York: Simon & Schuster, 2013.

McGrath, Declan, and Felim MacDermott. "Andrew Stanton." In *Screenwriting*. Burlington: Focal Press, 2003.

McKeon, Michael. *The Secret History of Domesticity: Public, Private, and the Division of Knowledge*. Baltimore: Johns Hopkins University Press, 2005.

Menand, Louis. *The Marketplace of Ideas: Reform and Resistance in the American University*. New York: W. W. Norton, 2010.

Metcalfe, Janet, and Walter Mischel. "A Hot/Cool–System Analysis of Delay of Gratification: Dynamics of Willpower." *Psychological Review* 106, no. 1 (1999): 3–19. doi:10.1037/0033-295X.106.1.3.

Miller, D. A. *Narrative and Its Discontents: Problems of Closure in the Traditional Novel*. Princeton, NJ: Princeton University Press, 1989.

Mills, C. Wright. *White Collar: The American Middle Classes*. New York: Oxford University Press, 1951.

Milton, John. *John Milton Prose: Major Writings on Liberty, Politics, Religion, and Education*. Edited by David Loewenstein. Wiley-Blackwell, 2012.

Milton, John, Ana Solodkin, Petr Hlustik, and Steven L. Small. "The Mind of Expert Motor Performance Is Cool and Focused." *Neuro-Image* 35, no. 2 (April 2007): 804–13.

Montaigne, Michel. *The Complete Essays*. Translated by M. A. Screech. New York: Penguin, 2004.

Moxey, P. K. F. "Erasmus and the Iconography of Pieter Aertsen's *Christ in the House of Martha and Mary* in the Boymans–van Beuningen Museum." *Journal of the Warburg and Courtauld Institutes*, no. 34 (1971): 335–36.

Nightingale, Andrea Wilson. *Spectacles of Truth in Classical Greek Philosophy: Theoria in Its Cultural Context*. Cambridge: Cambridge University Press, 2009.

Origen. *Homilies on Luke*. Translated by Joseph Lienhard. Washington, DC: Catholic University of America Press, 2009.

Orrill, Robert, ed. *Education and Democracy: Re-Imagining Liberal Learning in America*. New York: College Board, 1998.

Pack, Arthur Newton. *The Challenge of Leisure*. New York: Macmillan, 1934.

Paik, Karen. *To Infinity and Beyond! The Story of Pixar Animation Studios*. San Francisco: Chronicle Books, 2007.

Palmer, Parker J., Arthur Zajonc, and Megan Scribner. *The Heart of Higher Education: A Call to Renewal*. San Francisco: Jossey-Bass, 2010.

Panos, Robert J., Alexander W. Astin, and John A. Creager. "National Norms for Entering College Freshmen—Fall 1967." Washington, DC: American Council on Education Office of Research, 1967.

Paris, Bernard J. "George Eliot's Religion of Humanity." *ELH* 29, no. 4 (December 1962): 418–43.

Parry, Richard Lloyd. "Marie Kondo Is the Maiden of Mess." *Australian*, April 19, 2014. http://www.theaustralian.com.au/news/world /marie-kondo-is-the-maiden-of-mess/story-fnb64oi6-12268880 44451.

Perry, Ben Edwin, ed. *Aesopica: A Series of Texts Relating to Aesop or Ascribed to Him or Closely Connected with the Literary Tradition That Bears His Name*. Urbana: University of Illinois Press, 1952.

Peters, Thomas J., and Robert H. Waterman. *In Search of Excellence: Lessons from America's Best-Run Companies*. New York: Harper-Business, 2004.

Petrarch. *De Vita Solitaria*. Translated by Jacob Zeitlin. Westport, CT: Hyperion Press, 1978.

Pfeiffer, Franz. "The Good Housewife." In *Meister Eckhart*, translated by C. de B. Evans, vol. 1. London: J. M. Watkins, 1952.

Philo. *De Specialibus Legibus*. Translated by F. H. Colson and G. H. Whitaker. 10 vols. Loeb Classics. London: Heinemann, 1929.

———. *On Mating, with the Preliminary Studies*. Translated by F. H. Colson and G. H. Whitaker. Loeb Classical Library 261. Cambridge, MA: Harvard University Press, 1932.

———. *The Posterity and Exile of Cain*. Translated by F. H. Colson and G. H. Whitaker. Loeb Classical Library 227. Cambridge, MA: Harvard University Press, 1932.

Pieper, Josef. *Leisure, the Basis of Culture*. New York: New American Library, 1952.

Plato. *Gorgias*. Translated by Donald J. Zeyl. Indianapolis: Hackett, 1986.

———. *Republic*. Edited by C. D. C. Reeve. Translated by G. M. A. Grube. Indianapolis: Hackett, 1992.

Pope, Denise Clark. *Doing School: How We Are Creating a Generation of Stressed-Out, Materialistic, and Miseducated Students*. New Haven, CT: Yale University Press, 2001.

Pound, A. "Out of Unemployment into Leisure." *Atlantic Review* 146 (December 1930): 784–92.

Price, David A. *The Pixar Touch: The Making of a Company*. New York: Alfred A. Knopf, 2008.

Proulx, Travis, Steven J. Heine, and Kathleen D. Vohs. "When Is the Unfamiliar the Uncanny? Meaning Affirmation after Exposure to Absurdist Literature, Humor, and Art." *Personality and Social Psychology Bulletin* 36, no. 6 (June 2010): 817–29.

Pryor, John H., Sylvia Hurtado, Victor B. Saenz, José Luis Santos, and William S. Korn. "The American Freshman: Forty Year Trends." Los Angeles: Cooperative Institutional Research Program, Higher Education Research Institute, UCLA, 2007. http://heri.ucla.edu /PDFs/40TrendsManuscript.pdf.

Randel, Don Michael. "The Public Good: Knowledge as the Foundation for a Democratic Society." *Daedalus* 138, no. 1 (2009): 8–12.

Ravitch, Diane. *Left Back: A Century of Failed School Reforms*. New York: Simon & Schuster, 2000.

Richardson, Robert D. *Henry Thoreau: A Life of the Mind*. Berkeley: University of California Press, 1988.

Rodham, Hillary D. "1969 Student Commencement Speech." Wellesley College, May 31, 1969. http://www.wellesley.edu/events/com mencement/archives/1969commencement/studentspeech.

Rosenzwig, Roy. *Eight Hours for What We Will: Workers and Leisure in an Industrial City, 1870–1920*. Cambridge: Cambridge University Press, 1985.

Rushkoff, Douglas. *Present Shock: When Everything Happens Now*. New York: Current, 2014.

Ryan, Alan. *John Dewey and the High Tide of American Liberalism*. New York: W. W. Norton, 1995.

Rybczynski, Witold. *Waiting for the Weekend*. New York: Viking, 1991.

Sapolsky, Robert. "This Is Your Brain on Metaphors." *New York Times*, "Opinionator" blog, November 14, 2010. http://opinionator.blogs .nytimes.com/2010/11/14/this-is-your-brain-on-metaphors/.

Schlender, Brent. "The Lost Steve Jobs Tapes." *Fast Company*, March 30, 2012. http://www.fastcompany.com/1826869/lost-steve-jobs -tapes.

Schneider, Carol Geary. "Liberal Education and Integrative Learning." *Issues in Integrative Studies* 21 (2003): 1–8.

Schumacher, E. F. *Good Work*. New York: Harper & Row, 1979.

Schwartz, Barry. *The Paradox of Choice: Why More Is Less*. New York: Harper Perennial, 2005.

Seim, Turid Karlsen. "The Gospel of Luke." In *Searching the Scriptures: A Feminist Commentary*, edited by Elizabeth Schüssler Fiorenza, vol. 2. New York: Crossroad Publishing, 1994.

Selye, Hans. *From Dream to Discovery: On Being a Scientist*. New York: McGraw-Hill, 1964.

———. *The Stress of Life*. 2nd ed. New York: McGraw-Hill Education, 1978.

———. *Stress without Distress*. Philadelphia: Lippincott Williams & Wilkins, 1974.

Seneca. *Letters from a Stoic*. Translated by Robin Campbell. Harmondsworth: Penguin Classics, 1969.

Shapin, Steven. "The House of Experiment in Seventeenth-Century England." *Isis* 79, no. 3 (1988): 373–404.

———. "Personal Development and Intellectual Biography: The Case of Robert Boyle." *British Journal for the History of Science*, no. 26 (1993): 335–45.

Shepherd, Jessica. "Fertile Minds Need Feeding." *Guardian*, February 10, 2009. http://www.theguardian.com/education/2009/feb/10 /teaching-sats.

Shulevitz, Judith. *The Sabbath World: Glimpses of a Different Order of Time*. New York: Random House, 2010.

Siddique, Haroon, and Helen Pidd. "Anders Behring Breivik Trial, Day Four—Thursday 19 April." *Guardian*, April 19, 2012. http://www.the guardian.com/world/2012/apr/19/anders-behring-breivik-trial -live.

Siegel, Daniel J. *Mindsight: The New Science of Personal Transformation.* New York: Bantam, 2010.

Snedden, David. "Cardinal Principles of Secondary Education." *School and Society* 9, no. 227 (1919): 517–27.

———. "The Schools of Rank and File." *Stanford Alumnus*, 1900.

———. *Vocational Education.* New York: Macmillan, 1920.

———. "What of Liberal Education?" *Atlantic Monthly*, January 1912.

Spiegl, Fritz. *A Game of Two Halves, Brian.* Glasgow: HarperCollins Canada, 1996.

Stewart, James B. *Disney War: The Battle for the Magic Kingdom.* New York: Simon & Schuster, 2006.

Suits, Bernard. *The Grasshopper: Games, Life and Utopia.* Peterborough, ON: Broadview Press, 2005.

Sunstein, Cass R., and Edna Ullmann-Margalit. "Second-Order Decisions." University of Chicago Law School, John M. Olin Program in Law and Economics Working Paper no. 57 (June 1998).

Tan, Chade-Meng. *Search inside Yourself: The Unexpected Path to Achieving Success, Happiness (and World Peace).* New York: HarperOne, 2012.

Tapscott, Don. *Growing Up Digital: The Rise of the Net Generation.* New York: McGraw-Hill, 1999.

———. *Grown Up Digital: How the Net Generation Is Changing Your World.* New York: McGraw-Hill Education, 2008.

Taylor, Charles. *A Secular Age.* Cambridge, MA: Belknap Press of Harvard University Press, 2007.

Teresa. *The Complete Works of St. Teresa of Avila.* Edited and translated by E. Allison Peers. 3 vols. London: Burns & Oates, 2002.

Thomas, Douglas, and John Seely Brown. *A New Culture of Learning: Cultivating the Imagination for a World of Constant Change.* Lexington: CreateSpace Independent Publishing Platform, 2011.

Thomas à Kempis. *The Imitation of Christ.* Grand Rapids, MI: Christian Classics Ethereal Library, 1940.

Thomas Aquinas. *St. Thomas Aquinas: Philosophical Texts.* Translated by Thomas Gilby. New York: Oxford University Press, 1951.

Thompson, E. P. "Time, Work-Discipline, and Industrial Capitalism." *Past and Present* 38, no. 1 (1967): 56–97.

Thoreau, Henry David. *The Correspondence of Henry D. Thoreau.* Vol. 1,

1834–1848. Edited by Robert N. Hudspeth. Princeton, NJ: Princeton University Press, 2013.

———. *The Journal of Henry David Thoreau, 1837–1861*. Edited by Damion Searls. New York: NYRB Classics, 2009.

———. *Walden and Other Writings*. Edited by Brooks Atkinson. New York: Modern Library, 1992.

Tyler, Edward Burnett. *Primitive Culture: Researches into the Development of the Mythology, Philosophy, Religion, Arts, and Custom*. London: John Murray, 1871.

Veblen, Thorstein. *The Theory of the Leisure Class*. Edited by Martha Banta. Oxford: Oxford University Press, 2007.

Vedantam, Shankar. *The Hidden Brain: How Our Unconscious Minds Elect Presidents, Control Markets, Wage Wars, and Save Our Lives*. New York: Spiegel & Grau, 2010.

Vickers, Brian. "Public and Private Life in Seventeenth-Century England: The Mackenzie-Evelyn Debate." In *Arbeit, Musse, Meditation: Betrachtungen zur "Vita Activa" und "Vita Contemplativa,"* edited by Brian Vickers. Zürich: Verlag de Fachvereine, 1985.

Vives, Juan Luis. *Vives: On Education; A Translation of the De Tradendis Disciplinis*. Translated by Foster Watson. Cambridge: Cambridge University Press, 1913.

Wallace, David Foster. *Consider the Lobster and Other Essays*. New York: Back Bay Books, 2007.

Wallis, Claudia. "Stress: Can We Cope?" *Time*, June 6, 1983.

Watters, Ethan. *Crazy Like Us: The Globalization of the American Psyche*. New York: Free Press, 2010.

Webster, D. Hutton. "An Aristocracy of Achievement." *Stanford Alumnus*, 1900.

Weich, Dave. "Barbara Kingsolver Does Something Great for Her Country. She Eats It." *Powells.com*, April 24, 2007.

Welsh, Alexander. *George Eliot and Blackmail*. Cambridge, MA: Harvard University Press, 1985.

Whitson, Jennifer A., and Adam D. Galinsky. "Lacking Control Increases Illusory Pattern Perception." *Science* 322, no. 5898 (October 2008): 115–17. doi:10.1126/science.1159845.

Williams, Anthony D., and Don Tapscott. *Wikinomics: How Mass Collaboration Changes Everything*. New York: Penguin, 2008.

Winograd, Morley, and Michael D. Hais. *Millennial Momentum: How a New Generation Is Remaking America*. New Brunswick, NJ: Rutgers University Press, 2011.

Wolf, Gary. "The Data-Driven Life." *New York Times*, April 28, 2010. http://www.nytimes.com/2010/05/02/magazine/02self-measurement-t.html

Index